For the Love of Nadia

Sarah Taylor

For the Love of Nadia

My daughter was kidnapped by her father and taken to Libya. This is my heart-wrenching true story of my quest to bring her home.

JOHN BLAKE

Published by John Blake Publishing Ltd,
3 Bramber Court, 2 Bramber Road,
London W14 9PB, England

www.johnblakepublishing.co.uk

www.facebook.com/Johnblakepub facebook

twitter.com/johnblakepub twitter

First published in paperback in 2013

ISBN: 978 1 78219 015 8

British Library Cataloguing-in-Publication Data:

A catalogue record for this book is available from the British Library.

Design by www.envydesign.co.uk

Printed and bound in Great Britain by CPI Group (UK) Ltd, Croydon, CR0 4YY

1 3 5 7 9 10 8 6 4 2

Papers used by John Blake Publishing are natural, recyclable products made from wood grown in sustainable forests. The manufacturing processes conform to the environmental regulations of the country of origin.

To my beautiful princess, Nadia. She is a delightful and wonderful little girl and I'm so very proud to call her my daughter. She has been through so much and has come out the other side, always smiling. When she reads this book I hope she can fully understand why I did what I did. Nadia is my life and I will do anything to protect her.

I love you darling 'to infinity and beyond'.

Mum xxx

Acknowledgements

There are so many people that have helped me, given me the confidence along the way and encouraged me to keep going, and never give up. I hope I have included everyone, but please forgive me if I have omitted anyone.

First of all, I would like to give a special thanks to my wonderful parents, David and Dorothy Taylor, who have supported me throughout, never doubted me and made me the person I am today. They really are the best parents and grandparents we could wish for. I hope I am as good a parent to Nadia as you have been to me. I don't tell you both often enough, but I love you both very much.

To my brother Andrew and his wife Kirsty and my sister Steph and her partner Jamie for their love and support. Thank you – all of you.

My local MP, Andy Burnham, for his constant support and for keeping the governments in Libya and the UK on their toes.

Detective Superintendent Phil Owen for being 'my rock' and for being on the other end of the phone when I needed that extra push to keep going, and all the staff at Greater Manchester Police who were involved in Nadia's story.

While I was in Libya, the British Ambassador, Vincent Fean, and his wife, Anne, for always going that extra mile. You are a wonderful couple and you will be forever in our thoughts. Thank you.

Arvinder Vohra, Vice Consul in Tripoli. What can I say? Thanks for letting me cry on your shoulder and for your reassurance and honesty. The Deputy Ambassador Mark Matthews, and co-worker Farouk for their hard work and professionalism.

All the other staff at the British Embassy in Libya. Thank you for helping bring Nadia home.

I am so grateful to Sally, Abi, Sophie, Sammy, Sarah and Hussain for accepting me – a complete stranger – into your home in my hour of need. I thank you for that and your loving support all the time I was in Libya. I love you guys. Thanks to Anne Otman, Osama and Hadile, for being my second mum, for taking me under your wings and treating me like one of your own. Also to Hannah for coming to court with me and translating when necessary.

Fiona Ratib, Sue Bouhulia, Elaine Musa, Angela,

Paula for being my friends for your support and understanding and providing some much needed distraction from all the dramas!

My friends and work colleagues at Revenue and Customs for their complete support throughout. A special mention to Linda Clarkson for being there for me on the dreadful day that Nadia was kidnapped.

My cousins Lee and Simon Schofield and sister-in-law Kirsty for participating in the charitable parachute jump for Nadia.

Dave and Kelly Woodhead for organising the auction night.

Mum's works, Electrium, for the fun day they organised.

Dad's works, Rainford Solutions, for their collection.

Brooklyns day nursery for the sponsored walk.

Catherine and Paul of CP Mini Travel, for their donation.

Thanks to Andy Merriman for his help in writing this book and to my editor, Sara Cywinski, at John Blake Publishing for her assistance and guidance.

Contents

Foreword

There's an old cliché about ordinary people having the capacity to do extraordinary things. Sarah Taylor's story invests new meaning into that well-worn phrase. It's a story of hope for any parent fighting for a child against impossible odds.

Leaving a job, home and family in Wigan for Libya, with little more than the clothes you stand up in, takes a particular brand of determination and courage. As Sarah always said, it's what any parent in her position would have done. She's probably right, but the truth is that not every parent would have the strength of character to go on to achieve what Sarah did, and in the incredible way she did it.

My involvement began in late 2008 when Sarah's mum

and dad, Dot and Dave, visited my advice surgery in Golborne with Detective Inspector Phil Owen. Alongside reports of noisy neighbours or bins not collected, the story they began to describe stood out.

I will always remember my surprise when Dot and Dave told me how this young woman, Sarah – who at that point I hadn't met – had already secured, on her own steam, an audience with 'The Leader' and recruited him to her cause. There and then, I knew that this Sarah was a force to be reckoned with. She has that rare combination of fierce intelligence, with a genuine warmth and decency – qualities that never deserted her, even during her darkest hours, which explains why so many people wanted to help her.

The truth is, she couldn't have achieved it on her own and I'll be forever grateful for the incredible professionalism and compassion of Phil Owen, Ambassador Vincent Fean and his staff. They represent British public service at its best.

Sarah's journey was, of course, intensely personal but one of the remarkable things about her story is the extent to which the personal inevitably became entangled with the public and the political.

The backdrop to all of the events described in this book is a simmering Libya and Middle East on the brink of massive upheaval. It didn't feel like it at the time, but, looking back, I can see now that the timing of Sarah's fight was perhaps the single biggest stroke of luck she had. The co-operation we were able to secure between the

British and Libyan Governments on Nadia's case simply wouldn't have been possible, even five years earlier, without the thawing of relations in the middle of the decade. But it's also the case that, if Nadia hadn't been located before Libya was engulfed in the chaos of civil war, then there are real doubts over whether we would have ever got her back.

Just before Christmas 2011, I was invited to the opening of a new primary school. It was only when I walked into the classroom that I remembered this was Nadia's school. Seeing that confident smile from such a beautiful girl, and hearing her speak with the broadest of Wigan accents, will always be one of the most rewarding moments of my life.

Rt. Honourable Andy Burnham,
Shadow Health Secretary, February 2013

CHAPTER 1

In a Little Wigan Garden

Funny when you think about it, I come from an ordinary family in an ordinary town in Lancashire, but my life has never ever been exactly ordinary. In fact, it's been quite the opposite. Even my arrival, on 10 July 1976, was dramatic – my mum had been in labour for thirty-six hours; she needed gas, air and Pethidine, and was desperate to give birth, but I didn't want to face the world until I was good and ready. The doctor needed forceps to drag me out. It seems I've always been independent and had a stubborn streak – lucky for me, lucky for Nadia.

After a few days in hospital, Mum and I came home to 17 Chatham Street, Wigan. A two-up, two-down terraced house that my parents were buying from my mother's stepfather for £5 per week, it was small, but cosy, and in a working-class neighbourhood that was incredibly friendly and supportive. Everyone knew each other in the street and they were always in and out of each other's homes.

Mum and Dad met in a pub in Wigan and were only in their early twenties when they married. My dad, David, was in full-time employment as a welder, but money was still very tight. We couldn't afford to send our own car to the garage, so out of necessity Dad taught himself how to fix it. He then repaired other cars on the side to earn a bit extra. Mum, who worked as a seamstress, was equally resourceful. She bought herself a sewing machine with some money bequeathed to her by a distant aunt and made clothes for us. She really loved doing it, but she mostly did it as a way to save money without spending a fortune on clothes from shops.

When I was small, we used to spend a lot of time with my paternal grandparents. My dad was born in Wigan and his parents lived nearby. I remember spending many a happy hour helping my grandma, Betty Taylor, to make her famous currant cakes. Granddad Bill had a red Bedford van that he used to go to work in, and I used to stand up in the back and knock on the roof. Granddad would make me laugh by saying there was someone on the roof of the van.

My mum, Dorothy Bibby, was one of seven born in Singapore. Her dad, who was in Royal Air Force, died when she was just fifteen years old, so I never met him. She had a tough upbringing, and her mum struggled to bring up the family on her own.

In a Little Wigan Garden

Three days before Christmas 1980, my baby brother Andrew was born. Dad drove us to the hospital in our bright-orange Reliant Kitten and I remember seeing a doll in the boot of the car, all wrapped up in a big bag. Having sneaked a look, I wondered why Mum and Dad had bought a doll for a baby boy! I was quite jealous, but Dad gave it to me in the hospital and said it was from Andrew to me. I was really pleased and I remember thinking that having a baby brother was going to be fun. When he was about eighteen months old, Andrew moved into my bedroom and I remember feeling really excited about it. As the big sister, I wanted to be in charge of looking after him – it felt great to have this 'responsibility'.

Mum and Dad both smoked, and when I was a bit older they used to send me to Patterson's, a little shop across the road, for packets of Player's No. 6 – I think they were the cheapest cigarettes you could get in those days. The street wasn't busy and the shop was opposite our house, so my parents felt safe in letting me go there. Mr Patterson was an old man, who co-owned the shop with his wife. If Mum and Dad were strapped for cash, they allowed us to put any purchases 'on the slate' until we could settle the bill – I don't suppose there are many places where you can do that nowadays.

There also used to be another shop around the corner called Agnes's. I wasn't really supposed to go there as it was on the main road. The trouble was, this shop had a better selection of sweets than old Mr Patterson and it stocked my favourites – Jaw Breakers and Cola Bottles.

Luckily, I used to persuade Mum to let me go as long as I got back before my dad came home from work because he was much stricter about those things. I had to run there and back before he got home and caught me. He never did find out – well, until now that is. Sorry, Dad! There was another old man – Arthur – who lived across the road, and every time he saw me, he would give me a handful of chocolates, including Galaxy bars and Smarties. Sounds a bit dodgy now but it was all quite innocent, although I do blame him for making me into the chocoholic I am today! Looking back, it's surprising I've got any teeth left.

There wasn't any money for holidays when I was growing up, and I can only remember one trip abroad. When I was quite small, we were invited by my uncle Harry and his family to tour Europe in his motorhome. I remember the blazing-hot weather – Dad even got sunstroke in Switzerland – but, despite this, we all had a great time together. A few years later, Dad bought an old ambulance that he spray-painted beige and converted into his own form of motorhome. The vehicle had two beds, which converted into tables, a sink and cupboard space. We went camping to Flamingo Land in North Yorkshire, and Andrew and I would take ourselves off and play on the woodland park and the small theme park, which wasn't so extensive in those days.

As kids, we got on well. We used to play ball in the street late at night with our cousins, Mark and Michael. As I was the eldest, I would always order them around, although I think I might have done that whatever age I had been. Despite being a bit bossy, I was a polite and calm child, and I took everything in my stride. Mum and Dad were firm with me – they brought me up the right way, and taught me right from wrong. Although very loving and affectionate, they weren't keen on me being a softie. Even when I was sick, they never used to make an issue of it; they gave me the attention when I needed it, but they didn't overdo it. I'm sure their influence has made me the person I am today: they helped make me strong and secure and gave me a strict moral code to follow. Also, they were always honest with me and I like to think that I always try to be truthful and straight with people.

In early 1983, Mum and Dad decided that Andrew and I needed our own bedrooms, so we moved to another part of Wigan. The house at 18 Meadway was a much larger property; with three bedrooms and a front and rear garden. Our previous home in Chatham Street only had a backyard so my brother and I were thrilled that we now had a proper garden to play in. We really loved our new surroundings and felt happy in our relatively spacious setting. Unfortunately, this newfound bliss was not to last very long.

We had only been living in Meadway for a short time when I began to feel unwell. I was seven years old when a number of bruises started to appear on my arms and legs. It was very mysterious because I hadn't hurt myself. Every time someone touched me, another bluish-purple mark would materialise on my skin. At one point, Mum and Dad thought that I was being bullied at school and someone must be hitting me but this wasn't so, and, in any case, I had always been brought up to stand up for myself. I was also sleeping a lot and would come home from school, immediately curl up on the sofa and fall into a deep sleep. The bruises seemed to multiply and now my parents, who were becoming concerned, took me to the doctor. I was referred to the local hospital for blood tests but nothing of significance showed up. Then, one day, I was doubled up with stomach pain and rushed back to Wigan Infirmary.

I had further blood tests and a lumbar puncture. This involves collecting fluid from the spine. It's quite an ordeal for a young child and I remember lying on my stomach while various medical staff around my bed looked on. There was one nurse holding my hand, who told me, 'Squeeze my hand as hard as you like.' The doctor told me what she was going to do but I hadn't realised that the needle was going to be quite so large. I remember saying, 'But I thought it was just going to be like a pin!'

All these nurses and medical students were looking at me and, although I tried hard not to cry, I couldn't suppress my tears. The assembled throng all said how brave I was, and I felt proud of myself but I still didn't know what was wrong with me and neither did my parents.

The following day, Mum, Dad and I went to Pendlebury Children's Hospital in Greater Manchester, which has since become The Royal Manchester Children's Hospital.

We were taken to one of the wards, where I was shown a bed and asked to undress and lie down. Meanwhile, Mum and Dad were requested to go into the sister's office. A nurse attempted to put a drip in my arm, but I yelled at her: 'Don't touch me, I'm going home soon!' I wouldn't let her do anything without my mum being there – I suppose I always had a bit of an obstinate streak, but I was frightened. I was even more scared when my parents came out of the office. They both looked shaken and pale, and they were crying.

'What's the matter?' I asked.

'It's all right, Sarah,' my mum tried to reassure me. 'You're just a bit sick at the moment so you'll have to stay in hospital for a while but you'll be coming home soon.'

'But I don't feel sick,' I replied, 'I'm fine.'

'Please, Sarah – just do what the nurse says and you'll soon be home.'

Reluctantly, I agreed to let the nurse carry out the procedure but I was very unhappy. Mum and Dad stayed with me until visiting time was over, but then I was left on my own. I hated the thought of being in hospital, especially so far from home; I was being taken away from my family but, most of all, I didn't want to be ill. That night I sobbed myself to sleep.

At 1pm, on 8 August 1983 – the fateful day imprinted on Dad's brain forever more – the doctors diagnosed me with leukaemia. Soon afterwards, they told me I had cancer. I remember asking Dad the one question that he must have been dreading: 'Daddy, am I going to die?'

He took a deep breath, held my hand and looked me straight in the eye: 'Sarah, you know it's possible that you could die, but if you take all your medicine and do as the doctors and nurses tell you, then maybe you'll be okay.' He could easily have lied to me in an attempt to reassure me, but that was not his way. It's not *our* way.

He has since told me that it was like putting a sword through his own heart.

Right from the onset of my illness, Mum and Dad agreed that they would always tell me the truth, no matter what I asked them. They felt that it was important to be completely upfront with me, in the same way that my hospital consultant, Dr Richard Stevens, had been totally truthful with us.

It must have been one of the hardest things Dad has ever had to do, but his reaction and raw honesty actually helped me to come to terms with my illness and now, in later life, it has fashioned the way I relate to my own daughter. I am completely honest with Nadia and will answer her truthfully, whatever she asks me.

Anyhow, I was now in hospital and this was just the beginning of two weeks of intense medical treatment. At one stage, I spiked a temperature and was put on the critical list. My mum came to stay in special accommodation nearby. Kept isolated to avoid infection, I felt all alone and very miserable too.

The chemotherapy had many side effects; I was constantly vomiting, didn't eat and was being fed through a drip. I remember waking up and seeing a clump of hair on my pillow. Mum and Dad had talked to me beforehand and warned me that I was going to lose my hair, so I was kind of prepared for it. All the other children on the ward had gone through the same thing, so I expected the same outcome. Very self-conscious about losing my hair, I was concerned about what my school friends would say – I was really worried that I would get teased, too. Would I be bullied for the first time in my life? I was just hoping that, by the time I went back to school, my hair would have all grown back again, but it hadn't and so I had to wear a headscarf. (In fact, when I did return to school, some eight months after my initial diagnosis, the complete opposite happened: I wasn't bullied at all and I gained a lot of new friends, who were inquisitive about my look. I think maybe the school had warned them before my return, so they knew what to expect.)

One day, after two weeks of hospitalisation, my mum was in the kitchen preparing my meal, as she always did (I wouldn't eat the hospital food because it was always cold), and Dad was at my bedside when a nurse approached us. 'Do you want to go home, Sarah?' he said to me.

Before I could reply, my dad reacted joyfully: '*Do* we? *Do* we? *I* should say so!'

I was so happy about being allowed home but, as I quickly discovered, I still had to attend Christie's Hospital (also in Manchester) for radiotherapy as a day patient. As it was too far to travel, Mum and I stayed with a family who lived in Manchester and had a son the same age as me. Jonathan also had leukaemia and was a day patient at Christie's. During this crisis time, our families supported each other and became very close. Tragically, Jonathan contracted pneumonia a few years later and passed away. He was just a young man – I don't know how his parents ever got over it.

After I was discharged as an outpatient from Christie's, I had to return to Pendlebury but this time as an outpatient. Once a week, under general anaesthetic, I had a bone marrow test to search for abnormal cells. After a while, the tests were reduced to once a month, then once every two months and eventually once a year. I remember the doctor telling me that, if I was clear from abnormalities six times in a row, then I was officially 'in remission'. It wasn't until ten years later, when I was aged seventeen, that I finally received the all-clear, although even to this day I still have an annual bone marrow test.

After five years of my being in remission, Mum and Dad decided to try for another baby and, on 28 July 1989, my sister Stephanie was born. I was so happy that Mum had a girl. This time I didn't need to be given a doll – I had my very own living doll to play with! I could help dress her up and give her lots of attention. I don't think Andrew was best pleased that Mum had a girl – he definitely wanted a brother.

Everything started to look up: I was in remission, Stephanie was healthy, my parents were happy, and I was enjoying Rose Bridge High School, my new secondary school. I was regaining my confidence, making new friends and doing quite well academically. Growing up, I was very confident – I would speak my mind and always stand up for what I believed in. I liked to be liked, too, and I had a few friends who I really relied on – I always tried to fit in with the popular kids.

I was in my last year at school when I met my first love, Robert. I was fifteen and he was two years older. My brother Andrew played rugby and Robert's father was the coach. We had another connection in that our dads were work colleagues. Although my dad approved of Robert and his family, the thought of his little girl having a boyfriend was difficult for him. He didn't want me to start dating properly until I was sixteen; he also insisted that I was always home for 10pm and warned, 'Not a minute later, or there'll be trouble.' Dad wanted to know where I was at all times and, although it was frustrating, I knew it was for my own good. I'm sure that my being so seriously ill had affected his attitude and made him even more protective of me.

Right from the beginning of our relationship, Robert and I spent a lot of time together. In fact, we were inseparable. Looking back, I think we might have been a bit too devoted to each other and alienated many of our friends, who probably couldn't bear to be with such an exclusive couple. Eventually, it was only my younger sister Stephanie who would put up with our constant smooching – but only if it meant a day out in Southport or Blackpool!

After leaving school with nine GCSEs, I started work at Ormskirk & District General Hospital on an NVQ course. I earned about £60 a week as a nursing assistant looking after the elderly on a respite ward and I loved the job – I got to meet a lot of nice people. I had various tasks to perform, such as helping with feeding, toileting and bathing, but none of these responsibilities fazed me. Although some of the work wasn't very pleasant, I just got on with it.

I remember one old man who had just been brought in, who was very unwell. An exceptionally thin, tall man, he was always incredibly polite. He had been a patient before, but this time he was really sick and died a few days later on the ward. I was at his side when he passed away. This was the first time I had actually seen a dead body, let alone witnessed a death. I did all the usual stuff – I cleaned him up and then laid him out. I was then asked to open all the windows, which seemed to me a bit strange, but I was told that it was done to let 'the bad spirits' out! Millie Blake, the senior nurse, always insisted it be done after a death and I didn't want to argue, even though I didn't really believe in that sort of thing.

I was employed in the hospital for approximately eighteen months and, although the money wasn't too good, I loved every minute of it. Robert was earning more than me, working for HM Revenue & Customs in the Family Credit section, and suggested that I should apply for a job there. If I'm honest, I would have much preferred to stay on at the hospital and do what I was doing rather than office work, but it was better money. Fortunately, I was successful in my application and, in the same week, I started work as a civil servant, I not only celebrated my eighteenth birthday, but I also passed my driving test. Now that I had a better income, Robert and I enjoyed some fabulously exotic holidays together – we visited South Africa, the Dominican Republic and Kenya.

After we had been going out for about five years, and when I was twenty-one, we decided to buy a house together. We visited a show-home on a new estate and fell in love with the design. Our house hadn't actually been built, but we immediately made an offer. We moved in some months later and, with a lot of help from our families, bought everything we needed to set up our first home. It was very exciting to be moving into my own house.

Unfortunately, we had only been cohabitating for about a year when things started to go wrong. Robert and I had been together for seven years and, although neither of us got 'the itch', our relationship had become a little stale. I'm still not entirely sure why we split up. There were no major issues, or much arguing, but we had been boyfriend and girlfriend since our teenage years and perhaps we had become slightly bored with each other. We didn't seem to have anything to talk about, and we stopped having sex. Later, Robert told me one of the reasons why it didn't work out was because he was too young and he felt that he didn't have any space for himself. In retrospect, obviously neither of us felt strongly enough to make it work, so we agreed to part. Robert moved out and I stayed on at the house for a little longer until it was sold before moving back in with Mum and Dad.

Although the split had been a mutual decision, I was knocked back and, for a while, my confidence was affected. Fortunately, I had my family around me and friends to cheer me up. My friend Linda had recently separated from her husband and the two of us would go out quite a lot, enjoying ourselves. We met a few guys but there was nothing serious. I had just come out of a long-term relationship and wanted to have some fun and stay unattached. After all, I needed to make up for lost time!

Of course –and not for the first time – once things were on a seemingly even keel, I received another shock. Not long after returning to my parents, soon after the New Millennium celebrations, we were out having lunch when I rubbed my neck and it felt as if there was a bit of a lump there. Although I mentioned it to my mum, I wasn't going to do anything about it, but she insisted that I get it checked out. I had blood tests that were all fine and then a voice test. Nothing sinister was discovered, but because of my medical history it was agreed that I should have a biopsy and have the lump removed.

I was terrified that the cancer had come back and I was going to have more treatment. Unfortunately, my worst fears were realised when the results came back and showed that I had cancer of the thyroid. I remember the doctor saying that, if he had to choose a cancer, it would be this one as it is slow growing and can be sorted out without too much difficulty. Although this helped a little, I couldn't believe that I had been struck down again. Was I ever going to be rid of this evil disease?

After being admitted to The Royal Manchester Infirmary, I had surgery to remove my thyroid and both glands. I have always wondered if the thyroid cancer was caused by radiotherapy because the metal jacket I had worn all those years earlier to protect me during the treatment didn't cover my neck. I guess I'll never know, and I suppose it doesn't really matter now.

Shortly after the op, I returned to work at the Inland Revenue and resumed 'normal' life. At the time, I used to go out every Thursday night with my friend Lyndsey, who was an ex-work colleague. Both single, we'd go into town, taking turns to drive so that one of us could drink. We always started our evenings at a venue called the Chicago Rock Café because it was the first pub we stumbled upon on our way into town. It was a popular meeting place, very lively and played the sort of 80s music we liked. More importantly, there was a better chance of meeting someone there than in some of the other venues in town. Don't get me wrong, I wasn't desperate: if I met someone, then okay, but if I didn't, I didn't.

One night, in October 2000, Lyndsey and I headed out into town. She was driving so I didn't have to worry about sticking to the limit, although I've never been much of a drinker. On this particular night, the pub was especially busy but I managed to work my way to the bar to order the lagers. As I looked across the bar, I noticed a man looking at me. *Mmm not bad*, I thought. Although the lighting in the pub was dim, I could tell that this tall, dark stranger was also clean-cut and very handsome. A really good-looking guy, he couldn't possibly be giving me the eye. I could never attract someone like that.

Avoiding his gaze, I took the drinks to our table. Excitedly, I told Lyndsey that the guy seemed to be interested in me. I tried to play it cool but I couldn't stand it any longer and so I glanced back in his direction. Oh no, he wasn't there! He'd gone. I'd blown it. Suddenly I felt a tap on my shoulder. I looked up and it was him. Not as tall as I first thought, but still pretty gorgeous.

In broken English, which was a little hard to decipher, he said: 'Where are you from? You look Italian. What is your name?' Well, that was flattering for a start.

'Actually, I'm from here – I was born in Wigan,' I told him, all the while hoping that my answer wouldn't kill any possible romance.

I asked him where he was from and he replied, 'I was born in Libya.' That didn't help much – I'd never heard of Libya before.

'Where's that?' I asked.

'It's in North Africa,' he said, smiling. 'I am twenty-seven and a surveyor, but I'm here studying English at Wigan College.'

Charming, handsome and with a good job, this is going well, I thought.

He offered to buy me a drink and after a little conversation, he then enquired if I could help him with his English studies. I replied that I wasn't a teacher but I would be more than happy to help if I could. We swapped telephone numbers and he told me his name was Fawzi. He promised to call me in a day or two. I remember thinking that I would try not to build my hopes up. *Maybe we would just be friends. If he wants to see me, he'll ring me. If he calls, he calls. If he doesn't, then I'll move on.*

Of course, my reaction was quite different when Fawzi rang a couple of days later. I felt much more elated than I had expected – I was excited at the prospect of getting to know this foreign guy and learning more about him. We agreed to meet on the following Saturday afternoon, back at the Chicago Rock Café. I arranged to meet him in the afternoon because I thought it would be safer if he turned out to be too lecherous. Also, it would be less crowded and noisy, and I would be able to hear and understand him better.

When he arrived, I was pleased to see that he was as attractive as I'd remembered from that first meeting. He seemed at ease, talking about himself, and told me that all his family lived back in Libya and his property company had sent him to study in England. He added that he was a Muslim, and asked if that would be a problem. 'No problem,' I replied. I told him that we had a relative in Singapore who was married to a Muslim, and so I knew a little bit about the religion. It didn't seem to matter at this stage which religion he followed – after all, it wasn't as if I was planning to marry him.

Fawzi asked me if I wanted to go out that evening and, if so, could he bring his friend. I wasn't quite sure why he wanted to bring a friend along for the date – I assumed we *were* going out on a date – but I agreed. Although I didn't feel particularly nervous or insecure about the arrangement, I said that I would drive. That way, I could make a quick getaway if there was any nonsense.

I met Fawzi and his friend at a pub in the centre of Wigan called Berkley Square. The friend turned out to be his flatmate, Ibrahim, who had adopted the English name of Brian. Fawzi and Brian had been studying in England for about eight months. I liked Brian immediately and felt quite pleased with myself to be going out with these interesting and attractive men.

The three of us then went to a nightclub, where Brian busied himself by chatting up women, so Fawzi and I were left to our own devices. We danced and had a few drinks, although I was a little surprised that Fawzi, a devout Muslim, downed quite so much Jack Daniel's. Still, it was none of my business and we were having fun. We enjoyed our first kiss and I have to admit that I was already quite taken with his flashing dark eyes and dark handsome features.

Afterwards, I offered to chauffeur Fawzi and Brian to their home, which was a converted flat in a terraced house near the town centre. They invited me in and, although I didn't feel threatened – they had behaved like perfect gentlemen – I'm not naïve and, after all, I really didn't know them at all. I refused and said that I had to get home. Driving home, I was excited but trying to stay calm underneath. Fawzi had said he'd ring and, if he liked me, he would. There wasn't much more I could do, and I certainly wasn't going to chase him – that's not my style.

After a few days elapsed, I was still wondering if I was going to hear from Fawzi but then he called me. Thrilled, I tried not to let the delight sound in my voice. We agreed to meet at his workplace. To earn extra money, I had obtained a second job at the NEXT clothes shop in The Trafford Centre, Manchester, and was working two evenings a week and every Sunday. Fawzi was working in a pizza place in Whiston, near Liverpool, and I agreed to drive over there after work.

As you can imagine, it wasn't the most romantic of settings and he was at work, so it wasn't an ideal arrangement for pursuing a relationship. Still, we had a pizza together and managed to chat. Conversation came easily to us but he was working late so I didn't want to hang around and went home before he finished his shift.

We did this a couple of times and then one night I went back to his flat. Brian was there at first, but quickly disappeared. Fawzi and I had a few drinks and we went to bed. It was exciting and lovely, and he was very tender. As I drove home that night, I couldn't contain my feelings and wanted to tell the world about him. He'd already got me hook, line and sinker!

We began to see each other more regularly and, as I was still living with my parents, I found myself staying at his flat most nights. Very quickly I realised that I was falling in love with him, although I was a little unsure about what I was getting myself into; I knew at some stage he'd be returning to his job and family in Libya, and then what would happen to me? Also, what was he expecting of me? Was I just a casual fling? I was in a quandary because I wanted to protect myself, but at the same time, the more I saw him, the more I felt involved. It wasn't like me to throw myself in at the deep end, but my heart was beginning to rule my head.

After a few months, Fawzi surprised me by starting to discuss marriage. He told me that, ideally, his family would like him to be married before he slept with or moved in with anyone. *Bit late for that*, I thought. The trouble was, I soon discovered he wasn't talking about marrying *me*; this wasn't a proposal. It transpired that he was just considering the concept of marriage and how it related to his culture. Fawzi admitted that he hadn't told his family about me, and I felt really let down. If he was really serious, why hadn't he mentioned me to them? They probably didn't even know I existed. I began to think that if he was serious about me then he should be introducing me to his family. At least he could have told them that he'd met an English girl, who he was fond of.

It was all very confusing and I tried not to think about what some of my friends had been saying: that he was using me and that any thoughts of long-term commitment or even marriage – especially marriage – would be a very convenient way for him to obtain a British passport, enabling him to stay in the country. In any case, I was too fond of him to think that our romance was a cynical ploy on his behalf. This was more to do with his culture: his Muslim background and his religious beliefs.

There was also something else weighing on my mind. Although I was only twenty-four, I was already worried that my biological clock was ticking. I suppose having had two brushes with cancer had made me think deeply about my future. Life must be lived to the full because you never know what's around the corner. This may have pushed me to commit myself a little quicker than I might otherwise have done. The chemotherapy that I endured as a young girl might have caused me to be infertile. I was much too young to have my eggs frozen, something that could have been done then, had I been older. I'd been warned that I could start my menopause prematurely, possibly as soon as I reached the age of thirty. Now twenty-four, I desperately wanted children soon.

I couldn't afford to wait too long to commit to a relationship. I was thinking about IVF and even adoption. Besides, I was smitten with Fawzi, wasn't I? I explained to him about my medical history and the fact that I might not be able to have children; I didn't want to wait until we got more serious only to discover that he wanted to back out. I felt quite comfortable talking to him about this – it seemed the right time and very natural.

By now, I had introduced Fawzi to my parents. A total gentleman, they fell for him almost as much as I did, and maybe even quicker. He charmed them and nothing was too much trouble when it came to helping them: he came over and made typical Libyan meals for us. He even took Mum shopping. Mum and Dad had no qualms about Fawzi being a Muslim and loved him to bits; he became part of the family. Both Stephanie and Andy liked him, too, and got on well with him. They only lived five minutes away from my parents' house and so we all saw a lot of each other. There was a genuine mutual fondness, which made me even more certain about him.

I was still living at home, and Fawzi and Brian were still sharing their small flat, which was much too cramped for the three of us. Fawzi and I felt we needed more privacy, but I liked Brian and didn't want to see him kicked out so it was agreed that we would rent a three-bedroom house together. I suppose there must have been some hesitation on my part not to live with Fawzi on our own, which would have seemed more intimate and certainly more of a commitment. In some ways, it didn't seem like we were setting up home together, which was still a daunting idea, especially when it hadn't worked out with Robert all those years earlier.

This arrangement worked out well for about a year and we were extremely happy. Looming over us, however, was the prospect that Fawzi might have to go back to Libya in order to return to work, although he told me that he really wanted to live in England in the future. He said that he would need to return home to see his parents from time to time. Of course, I agreed that it was important for him to maintain his family links.

Fawzi returned to the subject of marriage soon after we started living together, only this time it wasn't a theoretical discussion: he was now talking seriously about the two of us getting married. He said his family were keen for him to start putting down roots, but he still hadn't told them that we were living together. I was made up.

I told Fawzi that Dad would appreciate it if he went to ask his permission to marry me. He agreed that it would be a nice thing to do and, of course, I insisted that I was present too. My dad's response couldn't have been more positive – 'That's brilliant, we'd love to have you as part of the family!'

Fawzi then went and bought me an engagement ring; it was very simple with a small diamond solitaire. It wasn't the most exciting or fancy piece of jewellery, but it was all that he could afford and I was thrilled to wear it. We wanted a quiet family wedding, and for our honeymoon we planned to go to Singapore. However, our plans were dashed in spring 2001 when Fawzi heard the news that his father had died suddenly. In Muslim culture, the deceased person has to be buried within twenty-four hours of death, and so, by the time Fawzi was able to return home to Tripoli, his father had already been buried and the funeral had taken place. He was distraught and particularly upset that he hadn't been around to support his mother.

On his return to England, Fawzi insisted that we bring our wedding forward and that we should forego our honeymoon in Singapore. He told me that it wasn't respectful for him to be seen enjoying such a lavish holiday so soon after his father's death.

So, on 10 July 2001, which coincided with my twenty-fifth birthday, I married Fawzi Essid Abuarghub at Wigan Registry Office. Fawzi had a few friends attend the ceremony and two of his cousins, both called Mohammed, were ushers. I wanted to have as much family there as possible to celebrate with us and, to honour my dad's mother, I wore the wedding ring that had belonged to my late grandmother.

Afterwards, we went for a meal in a pub in Hindley with a few friends. I have to be honest and admit that it wasn't the glamorous and magical wedding day that I had imagined when I was a little girl. Still, I loved Fawzi and it was all that we could afford at the time. Fawzi had no savings and so my family and I paid for it all. In fact, he didn't contribute to anything, but it didn't seem to matter at the time.

Some weeks later, we wanted something more to mark the event and arranged a party at Wigan Pier. Before the festivities, we actually had official photographs taken with me in my wedding dress and Fawzi looking very elegant. The party was a large, lively gathering, with lots of friends and family. There was dancing, drinking and a buffet dinner. I felt happier than I had ever been in my life; Fawzi seemed to feel the same way.

Everything was perfect and I was looking forward to a long and contented life with this lovely man.

CHAPTER 2

A Miracle Child

I was thrilled to be married and to begin with we were reasonably happy, although we were really strapped for cash. I had given up my job at the Trafford Centre but was still working for the Inland Revenue. Fawzi was studying English at various colleges and working at the pizza takeaway in the evenings, which brought in a little money, but I was basically keeping a roof over our heads. Fawzi claimed to be paying the Council Tax and would contribute when he could; he'd occasionally buy the food shopping or treat us to a takeaway, but it wasn't much.

I don't know what would have happened if we'd both held down normal jobs and were able to enjoy a proper routine, but within a few months cracks started to appear in our relationship. I'd go out to my office in Preston every morning while Fawzi was working most evenings in Whiston, so it was only at weekends that we were able to spend any time together. At weekends when Fawzi wasn't at work, I tried to persuade him to take us out for the day or do something different together, but, as he was working late during the week, he always seemed to be tired and not up to going out. I tried to be sympathetic and maybe every other weekend we would go into Wigan for a few drinks, then head home for a takeaway but, over the next few months, Fawzi began to act differently. He became distant and started to spend more time going out with his friends.

Fawzi was at home very little and, even when I was alone with him, he just wasn't relaxed – it was like he was nervous of something, or just didn't want to be with me. For some reason, he was preoccupied and I could never work out why, so I just put it down to his culture, in which all the men spend time together and all the women are either at home or in the company of other women. Perhaps he was just getting used to married life and this was how it was going to be for a little while. So, for the time being, I thought I could cope with this existence and hoped it would improve when we had children.

Having a baby was something we had already talked about and, now we were married, we could get going! I was desperate for a child and Fawzi agreed with me that it should be sooner rather than later in case I did have problems conceiving. But I tried my best not to dwell on this as I knew it would be much harder for me to become pregnant if I was stressed, but naturally I couldn't help worrying. A baby was what I wanted most and knowing there was a possibility of being denied this through no fault of my own was at times unbearable.

Looking back, I probably already knew that the relationship wasn't working out and believed that starting a family might improve things; I thought having a baby might change Fawzi and the way he related to me. I know it's an archetypal response and a little naïve, but that's the way I felt – I longed for a loving relationship and a normal family life. I had visions of the three of us going out together, just a regular family, doing everyday family things. That was all I wanted – it didn't seem too much to ask.

Before Fawzi and I were married I was using Depo-Provera as a form of contraception. I'd been having injections for a few years, but, as soon as Fawzi and I were married, I stopped taking it. My doctor advised that it might take me a while to conceive as a result of this method of contraception, irrespective of my medical history. My periods had stopped and so he prescribed medication to start them off again.

In September 2002, it seemed the impossible had happened: I thought I might be pregnant. I couldn't believe it and assumed I must be mistaken, but I did a home test and the result was positive. It's impossible to put into words how elated I felt. Maybe my dream was going to come true, after all. I told Fawzi that I might be pregnant but warned that it hadn't yet been confirmed by the doctor. He didn't react at all. Fawzi was never one to show any enthusiasm, but I was surprised by his lack of emotion. Perhaps he hadn't realised how accurate these home tests were. When I asked him if he was happy, he just said, 'Yeah.'

I went straight down to the surgery and was told to ring back a few days later. I don't know how I managed to get through those seventy-two hours, which seemed like a lifetime, but finally I was able to telephone my doctor and very nervously ask what the results were.

'Positive, I'm glad to say,' was her response. I wanted to scream with joy, but I was at work and somehow managed to contain myself. It was still early days, so I kept it quiet.

'How many weeks pregnant am I?'

'Four,' the doctor replied.

I felt so proud of myself. After all the fears of not being able to have a baby, I had done it. *We* had done it! I rang Fawzi immediately.

'Fawzi, listen, I've had the pregnancy results back. It's positive. I'm pregnant!'

There was a slight pause before he responded, 'Oh, all right.'

'Do you have anything else to say?'

Fawzi hesitated: 'Yes, that's good – *very* good.'

I was really upset when I put the phone down – I was so excited and he seemed so disinterested. I'd been expecting something more than this. Still, maybe he had just woken up; perhaps he was in a bad mood. Supposing he was with a friend and couldn't speak. Maybe it was as much of a shock for him as it was for me. Possibly he needed some time to mull over the news and get used to the idea of being a dad. *When I get home it will be different, he'll make much more of a fuss*, I thought.

By the time I arrived home from work, I was sure he would be there to greet me with flowers, hug me and make sure I was feeling okay. He wasn't working that night, so perhaps we could celebrate with a romantic dinner.

I couldn't have been more mistaken.

As I entered the house, he greeted me with a quick hug and a peck on the cheek, and then said he was going out.

I confronted him: 'I'm pregnant! Don't you have anything to say?'

After hesitating for a moment, Fawzi said: 'That's great, I've got to go – I'm late for work.'

And, with that, my husband was out the door.

I was shocked and upset: *how could he be so cruel? Didn't he know how much this meant to me?* But then I became angry: *I can't make him want the baby as much as I do, and, if he really isn't interested, then there's nothing I can do, but, whatever happens, I'm having this baby – with or without his involvement.*

I couldn't wait to tell Mum and Dad the news. Their reaction was naturally much more positive. They were, of course, ecstatic as they were sure I would never be able to have children and were thrilled for me. I didn't have to spell out Fawzi's reaction to them. They knew exactly what he was like and weren't surprised at his lack of interest.

Despite my previous health problems, I was really well during pregnancy and from day one I was blooming. I was very healthy and suffered no morning sickness. Completely on a high, I was excited the whole time. One thing that I remember about being pregnant was that, for some reason, I had a craving for melon and yoghurt. Late one night, I was so desperate that I sent Fawzi to the twenty-four-hour Tesco. I ate a whole melon and several cartons of yoghurt as soon as he got back!

Another thing that sticks in my mind was the fact that Fawzi didn't come with me for my first scan, which started an argument between us. He didn't see it as important and refused point blank to accompany me. Good old Mum came along with me instead but, when I got back to the house, Fawzi didn't even ask how I'd got on, let alone want to see the photo of the scan I'd brought home with me.

How could he treat his expectant wife like this?

Slowly, I was beginning to discover how his mind worked and how he would behave. If I stood up to him and we argued because of it, then I had to be punished – even if he was in the wrong – and then he would just ignore me.

I decided to leave the scan lying around the house so that he might pick it up and look at it when he was no longer angry with me. However hazy the scan, I desperately hoped that he would want to see the picture of our baby. *His* baby. I don't know if he ever did. At the time I didn't want to confront him because I knew it would lead to another argument. We were quarrelling a lot at this stage and, of course, the more we rowed, the more distant we became.

After each argument, it took longer and longer for us to start talking to each other again. The funny thing was, when we did make up, Fawzi must have felt guilty because he would be lovely and act like the old Fawzi I had fallen in love with. At times, I felt as much in love with him as when we first met. It was all very confusing.

Fawzi also refused to attend the second scan appointment, but reluctantly agreed to accompany me to the third scan, which revealed I was having a girl. I was delighted and my unbounded joy wasn't at all muted by Fawzi's lack of enthusiasm. I'm not sure it would have made any difference if I had been carrying a boy – his only comment being, 'Boys are easier to handle.'

I immediately went out shopping, and I couldn't resist buying some pink dresses – I probably bought more than I needed but I was just too thrilled to care if I was being silly.

When Fawzi and I did talk about our baby, we discussed all our hopes and fears, and even contemplated which school she would attend. Fawzi wanted the baby to be brought up as a Muslim. I told him that I was happy with that decision, but stressed that, once the child reached an age where she could decide for herself, it would be her decision as to which spiritual path she chose to follow. After all, it was her life and I wouldn't want to direct her one way or the other. Fawzi was happy with this.

Sadly, this seemed to be the only thing that Fawzi was happy about because for the next few months I hardly saw him. We were working at different times of the day and, whenever he did have an evening off, he would visit friends or make some excuse why we couldn't spend time together. The tension between us increased and, when I did tackle him, we would just end up arguing. Fawzi had a really stubborn streak and would always maintain that he was in the right.

It was so frustrating – he just wouldn't communicate with me and I wouldn't let him off the hook. The more I demanded of him, the more he reacted. It got to the point where he accused me of sleeping with other men. Mainly he insulted me with abusive language, calling me a 'slag' or a 'prostitute'. He even tried to get me to admit that the baby was not his. Our arguments became more and more volatile. One night, they reached near breaking point. I'd been out with some friends for the evening, and one of his friends, who had seen me talking to a male friend, telephoned Fawzi to say he had seen me out. Fawzi then accused me of having sex with this man and, when I denied these ridiculous allegations, he got me by the throat and hit me.

I was on the sofa and he got on top of me, screaming,

'This isn't my baby, you slag!' He punched me in the stomach and I was so frightened of losing the baby, I kicked out and he let go.

I realised that our relationship would never be the same, but, incredible as it must sound, I still loved him and I thought we could work things out. I tried to confide in Brian, who had known Fawzi since they were both at nursery school, and, although he obviously felt some loyalty, he was quite sympathetic and agreed that his best friend's behaviour was unreasonable. In fact, the two of them squabbled a lot of the time and Brian used to become frustrated with Fawzi. In the end, he stopped talking to Fawzi. Brian had lent him a sizeable amount of money and he never paid him back. When his English course finished, Brian returned to Libya, leaving the two of us in the house alone. I missed him.

I wanted to talk to my parents, but, although they realised Fawzi was spending more and more time away from me, I didn't want to worry them with his aggressive behaviour; I also thought I could handle the situation myself. To their credit, Mum and Dad had always tried to be fair to Fawzi, and they even stumped up some money for him to buy a car. Unfortunately, Fawzi didn't have any money to tax the vehicle and it was eventually towed away.

One night, while I was still heavily pregnant, there was some loud knocking at the front door. I went to open it and standing on the doorstop were two men. They looked Libyan, but I had never seen them before. One of them looked me up and down and then said, 'Is Fawzi here?' Fawzi was skulking in the background, but, as he didn't come to the door, it was clear that he didn't want to talk to these men.

'Can I help?' I replied.

'We need to see Fawzi,' said one of them. 'Is he in?'

I ignored the question and could see they were a little agitated.

'Do you know what your husband has done?' the other man snapped. 'We need to see Fawzi – he owes us money.'

Immediately I became defensive, saying, 'I doubt that very much!'

'We gave him money to give to our families in Libya.'

'How much?' I queried.

'£2,000.'

'There must be some mistake...'

'No, there is *no* mistake. The only mistake will be if he doesn't pay back our money. Then we'll have to take him for a walk, if you know what I mean.'

Fawzi had been to Libya a few weeks earlier, but he hadn't mentioned any of this to me. Before I could say anything else, he came to the door and told me to go away but I refused.

'I want to know what's going on.'

Fawzi was getting angry: 'Leave it to me!'

With that, he ushered me away and spoke to the men in Arabic. This time it was me who was hanging around in the hallway, waiting for the exchange to end. After a long conversation, they left and I confronted my husband.

'What's going on? You need to tell me what this is all about.'

But Fawzi just shrugged and denied any wrongdoing. He said that the men were being stupid and it was a big mistake. I told him that this sort of behaviour was unacceptable and that I wouldn't have strange men coming to our house and threatening him; we were both going to the police station first thing in the morning. He reluctantly agreed.

The next day, Fawzi refused to get out of bed so I decided to go on my own. I wasn't prepared to have this happen again and I thought that the police might be able to help, so I told the desk sergeant what had happened. Although understanding, he told me there was nothing that the police could do until something actually happened. I couldn't understand this as the Libyans seemed intent on doing Fawzi harm but there was nothing more I could do either. I was terrified that all this stress might have some adverse effect on the baby's health, but I also didn't want any harm to come to Fawzi. So I left the police station, intending to return home, but I became so worried that these men might carry out their threats that I went straight to my building society and applied to extend the mortgage by £2,000. I still didn't know if Fawzi had stolen the money from these men, but if neither he nor the police could sort this out, then at least I could.

That night, the two Libyans returned. I answered the door and explained what I had done to raise the money; I told them that they would have their money as soon as possible and for some reason they seemed to trust me. The following week, I gave them £2,000 in cash and told them to stay out of our lives. Far from being grateful, however, Fawzi seemed to expect that it had been my wifely duty to extricate him from this trouble and refused to discuss the matter further.

In the following weeks, he became increasingly uncommunicative and secretive. Then one day, by chance, I found out why. Usually I left for work by the time the postman called, but on occasion I was around to check the mail. On these occasions, I could see that we were receiving letters but they were addressed to people I didn't know, including quite a lot of correspondence for Fawzi's brothers, Fward, Ezzideen and Hamdi, who were living in Libya. On this particular morning, I happened to be at home when a letter dropped through the letterbox. The note was addressed to Fawzi and it was clearly official. I opened it and, to my horror, read that he was due to appear in court: the charge was that he was under suspicion of committing rape.

Fawzi was in bed and, although obviously desperate to know what was going on, I waited for him to get up. I then asked him, very calmly, whether he had something to tell me. No, he didn't, he said. So I showed him the letter. 'It's no big deal,' he told me. 'It has nothing to do with me – someone has set me up.'

He explained that one night, while working late at the pizza shop in Chorley, where he was now employed, one of the guys had taken a young woman upstairs and, a few minutes later, she came running downstairs, crying and distraught. She had accused him of attacking her and, unbeknown to him at the time, the man had apparently told her that his name was Fawzi. That's how he became implicated.

I was unsure whether or not to believe him as he was always good at worming his way out of things. I was angry with him for getting into such trouble, but didn't know whether he was capable of such a crime. When his court appearance came up some weeks later, I insisted on accompanying him because I knew he wouldn't tell me what had happened. He was more than surprised but he didn't try to stop me – I think by now he realised that I wasn't some sort of traditional housewife who was going to be blindly loyal and stick by him, whatever he did. Neither was I someone who would let things rest; I'd take on the fight – something he found to his cost in the years to come. I didn't tell Mum and Dad about the court case, as I thought it would only scare them out of their wits and they would worry unnecessarily about my safety.

Eventually, the case was dropped due to a lack of evidence. I had always believed in the principle of innocent until proven guilty but, with hindsight, I think he may have paid off the girl. It seemed strange that the case was dropped, just like that, but I still didn't know for sure whether Fawzi was indeed innocent of any wrong-doing. I contemplated leaving him then, but I knew what Fawzi was like and, if ever I really upset him, I knew he might punish me – and that might take any form.

A few weeks before I was due to give birth, Fawzi announced that he needed to return home to Libya to visit his mother, who was seriously ill. Naturally, I was sympathetic and fully supported my husband in his decision but I told him that he must come home within two weeks as I was due to have his baby and his responsibilities lay in Wigan, not Tripoli.

Ever since I had become pregnant it seemed that Fawzi had been struggling with the idea of commitment. Of course I was concerned for his mother, but it seemed to me that he just wanted to get away at such a crucial time. Although this may sound cynical, I noticed that his mother was at death's door whenever Fawzi may have felt trapped or vulnerable. And you know what? She *always* made a complete recovery!

Unfortunately, while Fawzi was away, I suffered complications in my pregnancy. I was still working about two weeks before my due date but one afternoon I had a routine appointment with the midwife. As usual, she took my blood pressure, but then her expression changed; I knew instantly that something was wrong. She fetched another nurse to double-check but she obviously reached the same conclusion. It transpired that I had developed pre-eclampsia (a medical condition which can cause hypertension) and my blood pressure was sky-high.

Apparently, I could have passed out at any time. They immediately rang for an ambulance, although I said I had just driven from Preston and could easily drive myself to hospital. I felt absolutely fine and refused to lie down on the stretcher, or go in the wheelchair. It was only in the ambulance, on the way to hospital, that I realised just how serious this could be; they were monitoring my baby's heartbeat and I was suddenly very scared that I was going to lose my child. My friend Lynette told Mum and Dad what had happened and they met me at the hospital.

In hospital, I was given medication in an attempt to bring my blood pressure down, but this was unsuccessful so the medical staff decided that my condition was serious enough to intervene. On the evening of 9 May 2003, I underwent an emergency caesarean. My mother was at my side but I was totally conscious throughout.

I had already given our baby the name Nadia while I was still carrying her. I'd seen the film *American Pie* and in it there is a beautiful actress, Shannon Elizabeth, whose real-life father was an Arab and her mother European. The character's name was Nadia. I'd always liked the name and, coincidentally, it turned out that Nadia was also an Arabic name. I told the medics what we had planned to call my daughter, and so, when my darling baby was about to appear, the doctor called out, 'Here's Nadia!' Hers was a truly wonderful arrival.

My gorgeous daughter had masses of dark hair and was tiny, weighing only 4lb 11oz. There were lots of tears and my mum, who supported me throughout, was absolutely thrilled. She rang my dad immediately and he was equally excited. I had dreamed of having a baby since I was a little girl; this was an experience that almost every woman is desperate for, and one that I thought I'd never have. Nadia was a miracle baby. She was exactly how I'd imagined her to be, and I was already in love with her. I just kept looking at her and picking her up – she was perfect, and she was mine!

Although desperately tired, I was too excited to sleep and I couldn't wait to tell Fawzi about his beautiful daughter, who had arrived nearly two weeks early. The nursing staff were incredibly helpful and let me use my mobile on the ward. That night I rang him but was unable to get through – not that unusual as it was often difficult to connect to Libya. However, four days later, I was still trying to get hold of him, which was proving impossible. No matter how many times I rang I could never obtain a ringing tone or even a voicemail response, so I couldn't even leave a message. It finally dawned on me that he had actually switched his mobile off.

Five days after Nadia was born, I was well enough to go home and my mum moved in to look after me. Fortunately, Nadia was a brilliant newborn and immediately slept right through the night, which made life a lot easier. Mum stayed a few days until I insisted she go home – I realised that I couldn't rely on my mum for the foreseeable future, and also, it wasn't fair on my dad. Besides, I needed to be independent.

Nearly a week after Nadia was born, I finally got through to Fawzi.

'I've got somebody here… it's your daughter.'

I was very emotional and, through tears of joy,

informed him that his gorgeous little girl had been born, but he seemed very unfazed by the news and not at all excited. He didn't even ask how we were, even though I told him about the C-section. I told him that I wanted him to come home as I still wasn't feeling well and needed help. He did at least say that he would try to get a flight as soon as he could, but I was really upset by his reaction and couldn't believe he could be so unfeeling.

I spoke to him the following day when he rang to tell me that all the flights from Tripoli were full and there was no way he could get back to England. Once again, I was really upset, but I believed him – I was sure that he would be doing all he could to get back to England. I tried to ring him again, a number of times during the next week, but there was no reply. Finally, I got through to him only to be told that he was still unable to secure a flight back. I knew Mum and Dad were pretty disgusted at Fawzi's behaviour, but weren't openly critical of him. They made sure that I knew that I would never be on my own and they would always support me.

Fawzi finally returned to the family home when Nadia was six weeks old. One night, at midnight, without any prior warning – not even a phone call – he just turned up. Nadia was asleep. Fawzi wanted to wake her and hold her, but I was so angry with him that I refused. I told him in his absence Nadia had developed a routine, which I wasn't going to disturb; she usually woke at five in the morning and so he would have to wait until then to meet his daughter. He wasn't cross, but didn't ask about the birth or much about Nadia.

For the first six months, I was on maternity leave and I did everything for her. Fawzi showed little interest and I don't remember him once changing her nappy – I don't think it had much to do with his culture; he was just too lazy or not interested. He barely played with her; he would give her about five minutes of his time until he became bored and, if ever Nadia started to cry, he would immediately hand her back to me. Although he showed her some affection, it all appeared superficial and not how I had imagined a doting father would behave.

There was little communication between us and he began to initiate arguments that would give him the excuse to storm out of the house; that way he wouldn't have to talk to me. It wasn't much of a relationship. I understand that men often feel excluded around this time and they play second fiddle to the baby, and I'm sure that Fawzi felt he was not getting any attention from me but he gave me very little and I suppose we were in the middle of a vicious circle that was growing ever wider.

All this frustration led to another bust-up. Fawzi had a fiery temper and, every time we argued, he would say the worst possible things in order to hurt me. He had, yet again, accused me of having an affair and this time I replied, 'You know it's rubbish – in any case, *you* were the one accused of rape!' At the time I was carrying Nadia and he pushed me, nearly knocking her out of my arms. Because of the previous incident – when he punched me – I immediately called the police.

Two constables arrived; one officer took him into the dining room while the other remained with me. I didn't know what was said, but, when the two of them came out, the officer told me that Fawzi had calmed down and they had advised him to go out for a while. The policeman told me that I should not hesitate to contact them again if I needed to. I was frightened that Fawzi might really hurt me and now I had to think of Nadia too. When the police left, I told Fawzi I would call them again if he ever threatened me with violence. I think that must have done the trick because, although he shouted a lot, it was the last time he was physically aggressive towards me.

They say love is a flower that turns into fruit upon marriage. Well, mine was rapidly turning rotten. At night I lay awake, tormented about what I should do. On a number of occasions, I seriously thought about ending the relationship. I wasn't prepared to play the role of the victim, but I was frightened that he would try to kidnap Nadia. It wasn't that I had read much about kidnapping, or knew an awful lot about children being abducted by their fathers, but by now I knew Fawzi all too well. I could match him verbally and return as much abuse as he dished out; however, he knew that I loved Nadia far more than I loved him and he realised the only thing that I could never recover from would be if he were to take her away from me. The thought was always on my mind.

After six months, I returned to work and Nadia started nursery. Fawzi worked on and off at a pizza place in Leigh, which was a little nearer home, but he had also been travelling back and forth to Libya for long periods of time. He had never been able to hold down a proper job or provide financially for us; I had always kept the home going by paying nearly all the bills. Believe it or not, we drifted on like this for two years. In retrospect, I was very naïve and kept thinking that things would get better. There was the odd day when we would go out as a family, which I loved and hoped that Fawzi felt the same way and it would change his behaviour. Mum and Dad knew how I felt and how unhappy I was, but I didn't unburden my problems on anyone else. It was only because I felt that Nadia needed her father that I kept working hard at maintaining the relationship.

* * *

In May 2005, when Nadia was nearly two, my mum's fiftieth birthday was fast approaching. She was keen to visit some family members in Singapore and so we arranged to travel to the Far East to celebrate. Surprisingly, Fawzi seemed enthusiastic about the idea and even offered to pay for himself, Nadia and me to travel there.

I was a bit surprised when Fawzi's friend, Khalide, turned up to see us off at Manchester Airport, so I questioned Fawzi: 'Why are you here? Are you married to Khalide or to me?' I didn't quite know why Khalide was there and was even more puzzled when Fawzi gave him an envelope containing some money, which he said was to pay some bills while we were away.

However, despite his initial eagerness to join in the celebrations, once we arrived in Singapore, Fawzi was very remote from the very outset. Clearly, something was on his mind that was occupying him. I asked what it might be, but he denied anything was wrong – 'Nothing. Nothing – everything is fine.' He wouldn't join in with the family's activities and couldn't even bring himself to take a dip in the hotel's luxurious swimming pool – instead, he sat on a lounger beside the pool, drinking cocktails and cutting a solitary figure. He said he couldn't be bothered to join in; he wasn't paying Nadia, any of the family or me any attention.

After a few days, I couldn't put up with him or his behaviour any longer; I'd simply had enough. And there was another thing preying on my mind – Fawzi had received a fair number of texts since we had arrived, and when I asked who had sent them, he replied, 'Oh, it's just Khalide.'

'What does *he* want?' I asked.

'He's just checking that I'm all right,' Fawzi replied.

'Well, of course you're all right,' I snapped. 'You're with your wife and family! Why wouldn't you be all right?'

'I know – I keep telling him that.'

But I knew there was more to it than that. Why would Khalide keep phoning or sending texts? I couldn't believe that he would be so concerned about Fawzi's welfare; something was up. The day before we were due to fly home, I told Fawzi that I wasn't feeling well and I wouldn't be going for breakfast. I asked him to take Nadia down to the dining room and said that I would join them later when I felt better.

As soon as they left to go for breakfast, I checked Fawzi's phone, which he had left behind. I checked his text messages first and there was one which immediately sent a chill down my spine: 'Call me urgently, or else I'll tell Sarah.'

I was furious that something was being kept from me.

What was all this about? What exactly did this person have to tell me? I took a note of the number and other numbers that I didn't recognise. Although hurt and angry, I assumed the text was sent by a woman so I decided not to make a scene and spoil my mum's birthday trip – I would just have to wait until we returned from Singapore before confronting Fawzi.

When we arrived home, I was surprised to see lights on in the house. I was even more surprised to see Khalide lounging on the couch, watching television. In fact, I was gobsmacked. Fawzi said that he had just called around to check everything was in order but it was clear to me that he had been staying in the house without my knowledge while we had been away. I am quite open to friends staying over, but why was all this kept from me? It was our place after all. We had barely put the cases down in the hallway when Fawzi said he had to go out and, before I could say anything, he and Khalide were out the door.

Immediately the front door slammed, I dialled the mystery number on Fawzi's phone. After a few rings it was answered. My worst fears were confirmed: it was a woman's voice.

'I believe you've got something to tell me,' I said.

'Who is it?' The woman's voice was slightly anxious.

'This is Sarah, Fawzi's wife,' I replied firmly.

The phone went dead.

I called Fawzi on his mobile and told him of my discovery. He was back in the house within ten minutes. At this point, I redialled the woman's number and put the phone on loudspeaker. The woman answered and I said, 'There's someone who wants to speak to you.' I handed the phone to Fawzi, who reluctantly took it from me. He looked as if he wanted the ground to open up and swallow him, but he managed to say, 'Hello, I can't speak – she's got it on loudspeaker.' He went into another room, but I followed him. Then he turned off the loudspeaker so I couldn't hear what was being said on the other end of the line. It mattered very little because he ended the conversation quickly and abruptly, saying, 'I'll call you back later.'

Calmly, I asked Fawzi what this was all about. He said he'd explain later and then just left the house. I didn't try to stop him or tackle him; he was so good at worming his way out of situations and very clever about thinking on his feet. No doubt he would come up with some devious explanation. I didn't think there was any point in accusing him of having an affair until I had some proof.

A few days later, I opened another letter addressed to Fawzi from Wigan County Court. This time he was under suspicion of threatening to kill a work colleague. I didn't know what to think – there seemed no end to the trouble that this man was getting into, but I really couldn't believe this of my husband. I rang my mum and the two of us rushed off to the pizza place in Leigh, where Fawzi was working. He wasn't there, but I knew Mohammed – the man that Fawzi had supposedly threatened – and accosted him: 'What the hell's going on?'

Fawzi had apparently become angry with Mohammed because he had invested £3,000 in the pizza business, but was seeing no return for his money. In a drunken argument, he had threatened Mohammed but it turned out that Mohammed had information that was much more interesting to me. While I was there, Mohammed told me that Fawzi was having an affair with a woman called Alison. I told him that I thought I knew who that might be.

When I got home, I decided to tackle Fawzi but he argued back that he didn't know anyone called Alison and told me that it was Mohammed who was having the affair. No matter what I said and whatever my accusations, Fawzi still denied he was seeing another woman and he soon stormed back out of the house again.

There was only one way to sort this out: I had to outsmart Fawzi so I rang Mohammed and gave him the number on Fawzi's mobile, which I presumed was Alison's. I asked him to ring her and then let me know what she said about Fawzi.

Some days later, Mohammed got back to me and said he had spoken to Alison. By now, she was clearly getting fed up with Fawzi's lying and all the intrigue. She told Mohammed that she had received texts from Fawzi and even Valentine cards that he had sent her. Alison also had an itemised phone bill listing all her calls to him at various times. She had agreed to give them all to Mohammed, who later passed them over to me. I think Alison was upfront about this as she had also become fed up with Fawzi and was now as angry as I was. I think he also owed her money.

I now had the evidence to challenge Fawzi but, when I showed him the Valentine cards, he denied having signed them and even said that it wasn't his writing. He also denied the telephone calls to Alison and said that he had lent his mobile sim card to Mohammed. Of course, this was all nonsense and I realised then that I was married to a compulsive liar. My head was all over the place and I really didn't think I could believe a word that he said. No matter what I accused him of, he would just deny everything. At times I even felt like I was going mad.

Just like the rape accusation, two years previously, this case was also dropped so that Fawzi was now free to leave the country. Then shortly before Christmas in 2005, he told me that his mother was ill again and that he had to travel to Libya. He didn't think he'd be back in time for the holiday celebrations. In a way, I was quite relieved. I told my parents that Fawzi wouldn't be with us for Christmas – to be honest, they weren't particularly upset. I also told them that I didn't want the situation to spoil the festivities – we were just not going to talk about him during Christmas. I really wanted to make it a special day for Nadia, then three, and I was determined that we were going to enjoy ourselves despite the effect that Fawzi was having on our family. Nadia didn't seem to miss him and didn't talk about her dad, but I made sure she knew that the reason he wasn't with us for the holiday was that he had to look after his own mother. I didn't want to turn her against him – even though she was still very young. I said that in the New Year I would decide what I was going to do. Mum and Dad told me that they would support me in any decision I made, but it was obvious that they hoped that I would end the marriage: they had lost the respect for my husband that they'd once had and they just wanted him gone.

While Fawzi was in Tripoli, I found correspondence in his coat pocket addressed to a woman called Alison. Well, what a surprise! I'm not sure whether I should have opened it, but of course I did. Both letters were sent from a high-street building society in Wigan. The first letter stated: 'Under the circumstances you have been suspended until further notice'; the other letter advised Alison that a date had been set for her industrial tribunal and that she was advised to have legal representation. I couldn't understand why Fawzi was in possession of these letters, although of course I now knew of his links to the mysterious Alison.

I immediately went to the local police station and told them that I believed my husband was having an affair with the recipient of these letters. It was pretty clear she had been suspended for stealing money from the building society. In light of all the letters sent to our address to men I had never heard of, I also suspected Fawzi of using false identities to obtain money. The copper on duty was grateful for my intervention, but said that the correct procedure was for my concerns to be reported to the bank in question. They should then contact the Fraud Squad, at which point the police might become involved.

The following day, I went to the building society and demanded an interview with the manager. She was taken aback that I knew so much about Alison. I showed her the letters I had taken from Fawzi's coat and another – an authorisation to give a credit card to Fawzi's brother, a man who had never set foot outside Libya. Fawzi was clearly impersonating him. The manager became more incredulous and took copies of the letters. She told me that she couldn't give me any further information about Alison as the matter was confidential and she really didn't know what was going to happen. I told her that I'd only be happy if Fawzi and Alison got sent down.

It had taken me a long time and I had been through so much with this man, but I finally realised that there was no future and, in January 2006, I decided to file for divorce. Fawzi was travelling back and forth to Libya and would disappear for weeks on end. I had no idea when he would return – or how long he would be back for. He would then just turn up late at night without any warning or explanation only to disappear again.

There was a long gap when he wasn't in touch and I went to see a solicitor. Fawzi couldn't be served with any papers because I didn't know where he was and so I was advised to separate on the grounds of adultery and desertion. My solicitor suggested that the next time he contacted me I should tell him that I was instigating divorce proceedings and I should not allow him back into our home.

Finally, after some weeks, Fawzi called me.

'It's over. The marriage is over; it's finished. You're not coming back to this house,' I told him.

He pleaded with me but I had made my mind up. I don't think that Fawzi ever thought I was serious about the divorce proceedings and he kept saying, 'We can talk about it when I'm back.'

A few days later, he turned up, suitcase in hand: 'Please let me in.'

'No.'

'Why not?'

'I've had enough of your behaviour – I've been giving it a go, but it's never going to work.'

'Let me see Nadia.'

'*No*! Now go.'

Fawzi stood there, all doe-eyed and sorrowful, but I remained firm and, when he realised that I wasn't going to allow him back, he trudged off. I don't know where he went – and I realised I just didn't care any more.

I got a real shock, a week on, when Alison called me and told me everything about the affair.

Although she herself was married, Alison had apparently been seeing Fawzi for eighteen months – even explaining that Fawzi had been late for Nadia's second birthday because he was with her. She described my house in detail and obviously had spent a lot of time with my husband there when I wasn't around; she also confirmed that Fawzi was blackmailing her.

He had threatened to tell her husband about the affair unless she gave him money, which she had stolen from her employers. Using his mobile phone, he had also filmed them having sex and threatened to show this to her family. She had given Fawzi £15,000 and said she owed the building society £20,000. It was clear that Alison bitterly regretted becoming involved with Fawzi: she was now in danger of being arrested and was desperately trying to get some money from Fawzi. *Good luck with that*, I thought. I think that's why she rang me – it wasn't out of guilt.

Funnily enough, I wasn't angry with her at first. I thought she had just fallen for Fawzi's charms in the same way that I had, but then the more I thought about it, the more I began to feel that she deserved everything she got:

she knew Fawzi was married, so it was her own fault for playing with fire.

In 2008, Alison was jailed for twelve months after pleading guilty to obtaining over £80,000 by deception.

* * *

In the summer of 2006, Fawzi and I were finally divorced. It was like a huge weight had been lifted from my shoulders. I was sick and tired of trying to work him out and I was ready to move on and live my life without him. I felt more like celebrating than crying.

Obviously, as a result of the divorce, access to Nadia had to be discussed. I agreed that Fawzi should be allowed to visit my daughter but I wanted him to have supervised access for his visitation rights. Unfortunately, the courts refused and decided that he was entitled to see her without any official supervision. I told them that he had committed the crime of blackmail but the criminal investigations were still being pursued and he hadn't yet been charged, so the court had to consent to his demands. Fawzi wasn't bothered about applying for joint custody – he just wanted access. It was agreed that he could have Nadia at his newly rented house in town every Wednesday for two hours and every Saturday all day, alternating with a sleepover every fortnight.

This arrangement went on for nearly a year and, if I'm honest, I have to say it worked very well. Actually, we got on better during that period than any other time since

Nadia was born. We communicated sensibly and politely, and Fawzi behaved himself. Nadia was only three at the time of the divorce so she didn't really understand what was going on. I told her that Mummy and Daddy wouldn't be living together any more, but that didn't mean we loved her any less: we loved her as much as ever. Nadia seemed quite happy spending time with her dad, but I was a bit concerned that his idea of entertainment was to take her to McDonald's or coffee shops with his friends. He never cooked dinner for her, never mind taking her to places that would interest her – it all seemed like a lot of hard work for him.

Fortunately, Nadia was loved, looked after and stimulated by the rest of her family. She loved my parents, who doted on her, and greatly enjoyed spending time with my sister Steph and her boyfriend Jay, who she adored. Nadia was a bubbly child and everyone at her nursery school loved her. She was such a happy little thing and was chosen to play a leading role in a concert – *The Litter Muncher* – that they produced at nursery school. I was so proud of her; we all were – she was the miracle child that everyone thought I could never have. The centre of our universe, she had everyone wrapped round her little finger. She was confident without being precocious, but at the same time she was also well behaved. Even at bedtime, she always did as she was told. I really couldn't complain about anything, she was just brilliant. We did everything together and we were best friends; she was just a very special daughter.

CHAPTER 3

Kidnapped

I was determined that Nadia's fourth birthday was going to be extra special. At the time, I remember thinking this would probably be the first celebration that she would be aware of, and the reason we were having a party was all for her. In fact, I started the festivities a day early and went out for the night with some friends from work, one of whom was an old friend called Mark. There was nothing romantic between us and we'd been work colleagues for some years. Fawzi never liked me having male friends – he would always accuse me of sleeping with them, whoever it was – so it was nice that I now had time to spend with friends, male or female, and just let my hair down. My sister Steph met up with us later. My intention was not to get too drunk as I had a party to organise the day after. However, I didn't stick to my plan and the next day I was a little worse for wear.

For Nadia's birthday, I had hired a double-decker bus, parked outside our house, which had lots of slides, climbing frames and ball pools – loads for Nadia and her ten friends to occupy themselves with. Nadia was due to go and stay with her father after the party, so I'd asked Fawzi if he would come and collect her a little later than usual, in case the party dragged on a bit and she wasn't quite ready to leave her friends. As soon as I made my request, I knew it was mistake. I should have kept quiet – he was normally late picking Nadia up, but of course, as soon as I'd asked him to be flexible, I could see in his eyes that for once – in order to cause trouble – he would actually be punctual.

As I predicted, he arrived early. Luckily, the bus had gone by this point, but a few of Nadia's friends remained at our house and we were still enjoying the party. I asked him if he would be patient and let Nadia enjoy the rest of the party, but Fawzi insisted she leave with him. He liked to show people that he was in charge – like he was the boss, the big man. Being in front of my friends didn't stop him; in fact, it probably made him act even more macho. He demanded that Nadia leave right away. I really didn't want to cause a scene in front of everyone and spoil her party, so I agreed to do as he asked. She hadn't even finished opening all her presents.

Nadia was naturally upset. She didn't want to leave her friends and also loved the attention, opening her presents in front of everyone and finding out what was underneath all the wrapping paper. It was all so exciting for her, but I could see what I had to do to keep the peace. I put Nadia's coat on and she left with him. Fawzi had remained calm because I'd obeyed him; if I'd stuck to my guns, he would have caused trouble. I was very upset after he left but grateful that I had my friends and family there to comfort me. Mum and Dad weren't at all surprised at Fawzi's behaviour; they knew what he was like and that he wanted to be dominant. They also knew that I had to handle his behaviour in the way I thought best and so, although desperate to get involved, they realised that if they interfered it might make matters worse.

A few weeks after her birthday, on Wednesday, 23 May 2007, Nadia was due to spend a couple of hours with her father, and Fawzi asked if we could meet in town. As we approached, he was counting a large wad of cash. He was making a big deal of it, obviously to show that he was 'in the money'. But it needed more than this to impress me, and I didn't like to think how he had come by it. I didn't even mention it, which I think annoyed him. Anyway, he seemed a bit cocky and asked if, instead of having Nadia that coming Saturday, he could have her to stay the day after, on the Sunday, as there was a Muslim festival in Manchester that he wanted to take her to. Nadia knew all about this and was excited; she really wanted to go and so, of course, I agreed. Why would I stop her from attending the event and having some fun with her dad?

A few days later, on the morning of 27 May, Nadia was up early, already dressed in her best designer gear – a Diesel dress and her Ted Baker denim coat. The girl was ready to party! Fawzi arrived on time, again unusual for him, but I didn't read too much into it. As I opened the front door to let him in, Nadia looked up at me and said, 'Mummy, I have tummy ache.' Those words would haunt me for the next few years, and probably always will.

I didn't really take her seriously and told her that she was probably just overexcited about the party. Could she have had an inkling about what was about to happen? Had Fawzi's behaviour been different enough for her to have picked up an unconscious message? In any case I hadn't been aware of any changes in his attitude. Certainly, I had no idea of the nightmare that lay ahead.

I remember thinking later that day that Fawzi had seemed a little flustered and anxious. Anyway, I helped Nadia into the back seat of the car and fastened her seat belt. I gave her a kiss and told her that I hoped she would have a wonderful time. As the car pulled away, she turned and waved.

That was the last time I was to see her for a couple of months.

After Nadia's departure, I thought I'd make the most of having a Sunday to myself. I still had my PJs on and decided to snuggle down on the sofa and watch some DVDs. By the time I'd finished watching *Pretty Woman* it was quarter past two in the afternoon. Whenever Nadia was with Fawzi, I would telephone her at 2pm just to hear her voice and know that she was fine.

Since the divorce and the custody order, I always had a feeling that one day he would try something. When Fawzi and I were together and we argued about everyday things, he would always do his best to hurt me in any way he could. He would call me all sorts of names as if he was punishing me. As I said before, he never used to like me talking to my male friends. At first, I thought it was nice and that he was being protective of me, his wife, but after a while I realised he was simply suffocating me and not allowing me any freedom. At the back of my mind, I always knew that he would one day want to get even, and that the only way he could really hurt me was through Nadia.

Anyway, I telephoned Fawzi on his mobile. After a few rings, he picked up and I asked to speak to Nadia. He told me that she was playing. I told him to interrupt her and bring her to the phone. Instead of doing this, he asked me to call back in five minutes. I agreed and then realised Fawzi had never done this before – he always put me straight on to Nadia whenever I asked. At once, alarm bells started to ring. I called back almost straight away, not waiting for any time to elapse. Fawzi answered immediately and told me that Nadia was too busy to talk, as she was playing with a woman. I had no idea which woman he was talking about. Funnily enough, I didn't even think about asking him – something was definitely wrong.

'How can a four-year-old be too busy to talk to her mother?' I snapped. I then asked if he had been following the news story about Madeleine McCann, who had been snatched from her parents while on holiday in Portugal, just a few weeks before. Having recently seen the news about Maddie, I had visions of Fawzi not paying attention, maybe being distracted by his friends or some woman or other, and Nadia disappearing. I told Fawzi that *he* should be playing with my daughter, not some woman I didn't know – the whole point of her going to spend time with her father was to be in his company. If Fawzi wasn't giving her attention, then he should bring her back and I'd play with her. Fawzi said his battery was low and that he would call me later. Then the mobile went dead.

I went numb with fear. Call it a mother's intuition, but I knew then that I'd lost Nadia. I had several contact numbers for Fawzi on my phone – some he didn't even know I had! I dialled one of them.

'Hello,' answered a woman.

'Who are you?' I asked.

'I'm Fawzi's girlfriend.'

'And I'm Fawzi's ex-wife. Where's Fawzi?' I replied.

The woman was very matter-of-fact: 'Oh, Fawzi's taken his friend to Manchester Airport – he won't be long. Try again in about twenty minutes or so.'

As I rang off, I was distraught. My heart was breaking. At this point, I knew for certain that Fawzi had taken my baby, the one thing that he knew would tear me apart.

My skin went cold. I can't explain why, it was just a gut instinct, but in that second I just knew he'd taken Nadia back to his home country and I might never see her again.

I called 999 immediately and explained that my daughter had been kidnapped and was, as we were speaking, being taken to Libya against her will. The policewoman asked how I could be so sure. I told her I just knew, and that the plane must be stopped. Later on, when I had time to think about what I could have done to prevent the plane taking off, I realised I should have called the police or the airport and said there was a bomb on board. I know that would have been a terrible thing to do, but, when something like this happens and you're desperate, you'll do anything you can.

I was told that they would send a police officer round as soon as they could. She then asked how long Nadia had been missing and I replied, 'Since 10am this morning.' I then shouted, 'Why does that matter? Nadia is on a plane to Libya, and I need that plane stopped.'

I was beside myself with worry, sickness, panic, hatred, fear. You name it – I was going through every conceivable emotion. I was alone; Mum and Dad were away in their caravan in the Lake District. Powerless, I sobbed uncontrollably.

I called my sister Steph. She and her partner Jay were shopping in town and she thought the call from me was going to be a request to meet up with Nadia because the three of them used to spend a lot of time together at weekends. Instead, I managed to splutter, 'Steph, come to mine – it's an emergency!' Of course, she got a terrible shock, but they rushed over immediately.

When they arrived, I was screaming: 'He's taken her, Steph – he's taken her! Fawzi has taken my baby!'

Steph started crying straight away. I knew she couldn't imagine life without Nadia, who she adored, and Nadia felt the same way about her. As soon as she saw her auntie, she would jump into her arms and give her the loveliest smile.

Once she had got over the initial shock, Steph tried to calm me down but I couldn't communicate properly, apart from managing to phone my friend Linda, who also came over to the house as soon as she heard the news. I wasn't up to speaking to Mum or Dad, so I asked Linda to call and explain what I thought had happened. Although horrified, they were not really all that surprised at what Fawzi had done. After quickly throwing everything into the caravan, they hooked it to the car and drove well over the speed limit on the way to my house. It was a good job the police didn't spot them on the way because Dad would have lost his licence, bouncing the caravan around at 80 miles an hour! Mum told me later that they barely spoke on the journey home – they were filled with fear and trepidation that Nadia really had been kidnapped.

The police arrived a few hours after I had reported Nadia missing. Although I explained again what had happened, they didn't seem completely convinced by my story. I suppose they thought that it happens all the time – fathers taking their children out and losing track of time. But I knew exactly what Fawzi had done; I knew him better than he knew himself. I had done everything in my power to put obstacles in his way, to stop him taking Nadia, but he'd tricked me. I'd let myself and my family down, but most of all I'd let Nadia down.

I gave the police a full description of Nadia, including what she was wearing and her distinguishing marks. As I was answering all their questions, I was having ridiculous, irrational thoughts: why were the police asking me all these questions, they seemed so unnecessary. I had told them what had happened and yet they were still asking for more and more personal details about Nadia. It didn't make sense. *Do they know more about Nadia's plight than they are letting on?* I kept thinking. *Surely they only ask people in my situation this sort of thing when a child has been murdered?* Already I was beginning to panic and lose my mind.

I asked a policewoman what she thought my chances might be of getting Nadia back. Could the police inform the aircrew on the plane that Fawzi had taken Nadia out the country illegally? Might he be refused entry into Libya if the authorities there knew what he had done? Either the police didn't know the answers to my increasingly desperate questions, or they didn't want to tell me. I kept telling them to be 100 per cent honest with me, and, if they had heard any bad news, I needed to know but no answers were forthcoming. I knew I had no choice but to wait, and to try to remain calm.

By now, Mum and Dad had arrived home. As soon as

I saw them, I broke down and became a child myself, losing myself in their loving and protective hugs. I sobbed and kept saying, 'I just want my baby home! I just want my baby home!' My parents tried to stay strong for me as they themselves came to terms with what had happened but I knew that they would do their crying in private, where I couldn't see their despair. We had to wait for confirmation that Nadia had arrived in Libya, as there was still a possibility that Fawzi hadn't taken her there, but I knew for sure – 100 per cent – he had. The hours went by, but there was no news.

While we were waiting, I also called Fawzi's friend, Brian, to see if he knew anything about what had happened. He answered quickly and I blurted out: 'Brian, are you with Fawzi? He's taken Nadia to Libya!'

Brian said he wasn't with Fawzi, and told me that they had gone to Singapore. I called him a liar and hung up the phone – I knew it was rubbish. Fawzi didn't know anyone in Singapore; besides, he needed a visa and a sponsor. When we visited there a few years previously, I remember waiting weeks for Fawzi's visa: my uncle in Singapore had had to sponsor him.

Speaking to Brian confirmed my worst fears. I was sure that he and Fawzi had planned this, and that Nadia was now in Libya. I kept saying things like, 'Nadia will be frightened – she won't understand what the Libyans are saying. She doesn't speak Arabic. She will be asking all sorts of questions and I'm not there to help her. What will she think of me?' Every time I thought of how lonely and distressed Nadia must be feeling, I broke down sobbing uncontrollably, and no matter how much my family and Linda tried to comfort me, I was too panic-stricken: I just wanted to hold Nadia and tell her everything was going to be okay. That's what mummies are meant to do, and I couldn't.

A policewoman stayed with me for what seemed like hours until a detective arrived at my house and confirmed that the names of Nadia Fawzi and Fawzi Abuarghub appeared on the passenger list on the 2.20pm Libyan Airlines flight to Tripoli. They were definitely on the flight. I was given a slight hope that the girl with Fawzi wasn't Nadia as her name had been misspelt, but I knew in my heart that I was grasping at straws.

At midnight, I was advised by a detective that they had studied the airport CCTV footage and had confirmed that Nadia and her dad had boarded the flight. When I saw the footage some weeks later, it was even harder to bear. I could see Nadia looking completely bewildered and, at one stage, she actually tries to return through the metal detector from which she has just been screened in a last disorientated attempt not to get on that plane.

I didn't think I had any more tears to shed but, with this awful realisation, we all cried hysterically. Steph was heartbroken – she had been a brilliant auntie to Nadia and couldn't believe what had happened. When we finally stopped crying, we sat in silence for a while before the questions started again. Steph, who despite everything had enjoyed quite a good relationship with Fawzi, kept asking, 'Why? *Why*? How could he do something so horrible? How could he do this to our family?'

The day before Nadia was snatched, my brother Andy and his fiancée, Kirsty, had taken her shopping for a bridesmaid's dress as she was due to play an important role in their wedding on 29 June. I told Andy and Kirsty straight away what had happened – Andy had wanted to go immediately to the airport to search for Fawzi and Nadia and stop them from boarding the aircraft. Although he would have been already too late, this is something he regrets to this day. (From the beginning, Andy and Kirsty were brilliant and actually took money from their wedding fund to buy me a computer and IT equipment, as they thought it might help in trying to communicate with Fawzi.)

Mum and Linda stayed the night, although I really just wanted to be alone. I couldn't go to bed that night – I knew I wouldn't sleep a wink. I just sat by the window in case the police had been mistaken and Nadia hadn't been taken. Maybe, sometime during the night, there would be a knock at the door and my darling would be home with me, where she belonged. But it didn't happen. This was a mother's worst fear and it hadn't happened to someone I had read about, or to a friend: it had happened to me. My daughter, who I worshipped and loved with every inch of my being and all my heart, had been kidnapped. I kept up a night-time vigil for as long as I can remember, for many, many nights.

* * *

Kidnapped

The following morning I had to call Nadia's nursery and tell them that she wouldn't be in that day. Usually parents call in and say their child is sick, or has a cold or is just over-tired; I was ringing the nursery to inform the staff that my child had been abducted. I could hardly get the words out and broke down for what seemed like the hundredth time since I'd discovered Nadia had been taken away from me. Through my tears, I managed to tell the nursery worker that I would keep them informed of any news.

Nadia was due to play a leading role in a nursery production, *The Litter Muncher*, in a few weeks. In fact, she herself was actually the 'litter muncher' and was so proud of having such an important part. I prayed that she would be back in time and hoped that Fawzi had just taken her to Libya for a holiday. If I could really believe this, maybe I might be able to handle not seeing her for a couple of weeks.

I naturally kept calling Fawzi's mobile and finally, twelve hours later, he answered. Although anxious, angry and terrified all at the same time, I was more frightened of hearing him tell me that they weren't coming home; he now had all the power so I had to hold a candle to the Devil and remain composed. I knew I had to stay calm: if I shouted or got angry, it would give him an excuse to say he wasn't coming home. He never explained himself then, and he never did afterwards either.

Straight away, I asked to speak to Nadia – I was desperate to hear her voice, to make sure she was okay and to reassure her that I'd see her soon. But Fawzi wouldn't let me talk to her: he said she was sleeping and that he wasn't going to disturb her. I had to agree because I knew, if I was more insistent, he would hang up and I would not be able to speak to her. There was also the possibility that he might buy a new sim card, and I wouldn't have any way of contacting Nadia. Later on, I discovered that he decided not to change his mobile number as he was anxious to keep in touch with me in order to know what I was planning.

I finally asked why he'd taken her and he just said, 'We'll be back soon,' and then he hung up. Those words didn't reassure me because I didn't trust him – after all, I had many reasons not to believe a word he said.

The day after Nadia had been taken from me, the police came to see me again. They advised me to speak to a lawyer, to find out about my legal rights and what action I could take. At about the same time, I had a telephone call from a woman from Re-Unite, a charity specialising in child abduction. She explained to me that every year over 500 children go missing and the charity helps mothers or fathers reunite with their siblings. Re-Unite is there to provide help and support; it's also a shoulder to cry on.

'How many children have been returned to England from Libya and been reunited with their mothers?' I asked.

Her response was chilling. 'None,' she said.

She went on to explain that it was nearly always Libyan

men who snatched their children. It could be arranged for the mothers to visit their children in Libya, but the fathers would not allow them to come back to the UK. At that point, I didn't want to listen any more; it was exactly what I didn't want to hear. I wasn't prepared to listen to anything like that. *Nadia will come home!* If this woman was trying to reassure me, she couldn't have done a worse job, although I suppose, looking back, she was being honest – something I had demanded from the police.

I was becoming increasingly agitated. I would fight for Nadia if it was the last thing I did. It might be a difficult journey ahead, but the shock and sorrow I had initially felt was now tempered by anger and a determination to return my daughter to where she belonged. The woman at Re-Unite gave me the number for a lawyer who specifically dealt with abducted children, based in Sheffield. She also told me that, if I ever wanted to speak to Re-Unite, any time – day or night – I should telephone them, but I never did.

I did, however, ring the lawyer and I informed her how desperate I was. She agreed to meet me the following day. My cousin Becky took Mum and I across the border to Yorkshire to meet her. The solicitor advised me to make Nadia a Ward of Court, but it couldn't be done that day as it was too late. A few days later, Dad arranged another appointment and Nadia was duly made the subject of a wardship order. This was all very well and might provide a safeguard in the future, but it wasn't going to help me get Nadia back.

The police asked me for any information I could provide that might help in the investigation. Although Fawzi hadn't been living with me for some time, I ransacked the house, searching for documentation that might provide a clue to his intentions. During my search, I found photocopies of ten different individuals' passports, including his two brothers. Although I'd had my suspicions about Fawzi committing fraud, it now seemed certain that he had been 'borrowing' money from the building society under false pretences: we discovered that he was nearly £50,000 in debt. Mum, Dad and I even searched my old shed and came across many telephone numbers in Fawzi's handwriting, which I kept just in case we needed them later.

Meanwhile, the police had advised me that, although Fawzi was guilty of kidnapping Nadia, there was very little – actually nothing – they could do. The only hope was for me to continue in my attempts to contact him and to persuade him to return Nadia. Of course, I was doing this all the time. Fawzi would answer the telephone to me, but refused to put Nadia on the line. He always made some excuse: she was out, or asleep or unavailable for some reason. People might wonder how I didn't go mad, scream at him and lose my temper, but I tried to stay in control of my emotions. I decided it was best to play my part very coolly to try to get Fawzi on side in the hope that he might see sense and at least let me speak to Nadia. It was very calculating on my part, but I thought I knew the best way to handle him and this would pay dividends in the end. Looking back, I don't know how I managed to stay in control sometimes when I spoke to him.

Finally, after about six weeks of constant ringing and totally unsatisfactory and frustrating conversations with Fawzi, he agreed to let me talk to Nadia. As strong and composed as I'd been up until then, I started shaking: I had to be brave and strong for my daughter.

'Hello, darling,' I said. 'How are you?'

At last I heard her sweet voice but her words broke my heart: 'Hello, Mummy, I'm in Libbiba, I want to come home, Mummy!'

Somehow I held back the tears as I told her that I knew she wanted to come home, but that she had to be brave for Mummy. I promised that I would see her soon. Before I could say any more, Fawzi snatched the mobile from Nadia and the line went dead. Then I let my emotions go completely and sobbed uncontrollably for hours. My baby was desperate to see me and I could do nothing. I just wanted to go to her, and hold her and tell her everything would be okay, but, most of all, I wanted to rescue her, yet I couldn't. I was helpless and there was nothing my family, the police or the law could do. Steph was there for me but later she told me that she felt as if her heart had been ripped out. At the time she wanted to protect me from how desperate she herself felt, though.

Losing Nadia naturally affected my whole life and dominated everything; it was all I could think of. I took time off work and my employers were very sympathetic under the circumstances when I told them that I had no idea when I might return. Instead, I wanted to put all my energy into bringing Nadia home and I spent every waking moment planning how to do just that. I barely left the house, wanting to be close to Nadia's clothes and toys. Mum took three weeks off work to be with me, but Dad still had to bring in the money. My parents were very supportive of me and we would sit there for hours, thinking about every eventuality. Steph couldn't go to college for a couple of weeks as she was unable to concentrate on her work and wanted to be by my side at all times.

My dad tried to speak to Fawzi. The two men had got on reasonably well and, in the past, my husband had been quite respectful – I presumed it was a macho thing. Fawzi had some old-fashioned patriarchal attitudes – mainly due to his culture – and he considered Dad to be the head of our family. Through gritted teeth, my dad would attempt to humour Fawzi with a laddish type of manner and, although Fawzi listened, he never made any promises. I was strangely optimistic because Fawzi never said he wasn't coming home, so I remained hopeful.

During this time, I was a total mess. I would sit by the window on a big Buddha bag (a large cushion on which Nadia used to love sitting with me), snuggling and stroking one of Nadia's blankets, crying the whole time. If I heard footsteps outside the house, I would leap up and look to see who it was – just in case Fawzi had had a change of heart and brought Nadia back home. Crazy, I know, but it was all the hope I had at that time.

I didn't go to the doctor as I didn't want any medication. When I'm stressed, my body copes by closing down a little with the result that I sleep a lot. I suppose it's a way of shutting all the horrible things out. Although I was sleeping okay, I was so wound up during the day that I was exhausted, just running on adrenaline.

By now, the press had got hold of my story and I received a call from the *Wigan Evening Post* to see if they could do a piece on Nadia. At first, I was uncertain because I wasn't sure how I wanted things to go. Should I keep everything quiet and do it my way, or should I go public and make everyone aware of what happened? Maybe it would help force Fawzi to bring Nadia home. I decided to tell my story to the local newspaper, and a few hours later a journalist came over to interview me. I had to retell the whole scenario again. Luckily, the reporter was very sympathetic and I was remarkably calm. I suppose I just wanted the whole world to know what had happened. It seemed at the time to me that the more people who knew the story, the more chance I had of getting her back. In the coming weeks, I would be narrating the story over and over again, and the more I heard myself talking about Nadia's kidnapping, the more determined I became to see my daughter and bring her home.

Unlike my interview with the journalist in which I divulged everything, Fawzi gave very little away in our telephone conversations. There was, however, one thing that worried me and confirmed that he had little intention of acting reasonably: he admitted having enrolled Nadia into a local school. I really hadn't wanted to hear this as he was clearly putting the whole situation on a more permanent footing. It was equally clear that Nadia wasn't coming home any time soon.

I spoke to Nadia about once every three to four weeks after she was taken. After every phone call to Libya, I was in floods of tears, my heart ripped in two. I just wanted to hold my baby and tell her everything would be okay. Whenever I asked Fawzi if he was bringing Nadia home, he would just say, 'I don't know.' I wanted to scream at him and tell him that he was despicable and that I hated him but I couldn't: I had to remain calm for Nadia.

The police put me in touch with the International Social Services (ISS). I had assumed that I could fly to Libya and bring Nadia home but I soon discovered during my first contact with them that Libya is not signed up to the Hague Convention or the European Convention, which protects parental rights and allows a parent to demand their child is returned. It meant that my only options were to move to Libya and launch a petition to have Nadia returned, or to try mediation and attempt to convince Fawzi to allow me access to my daughter.

In June 2007, several weeks after Nadia had been snatched, I had a call from Marek, who worked for the International Social Services. He explained that every year the organisation arranged a trip for the mothers of abducted children to spend a fortnight with their offspring; it would be an opportunity to possibly spend some time with Nadia. 'A sort of two-week holiday' was how he described it. I said it sounded great but asked what would happen when the fortnight was over. He told me that I would have to say goodbye to Nadia until the following year.

My immediate thought was that there was no way that I would accept this arrangement, but I could use it to try to work on Fawzi, to convince him that we could reconcile our marriage. Perhaps I could make him believe that I would give him another chance, although that was obviously out of the question. I was willing to try anything to get Nadia home.

I told Marek that I didn't have the funds to go to Libya at that time but he informed me that all expenses would be paid for by the ISS, so I immediately agreed to his suggestion. My family were thrilled and at last something was happening. The trip was planned for July so I had about a month to wait. I started counting off the days. It was agony so I tried to keep myself busy until then. I was still getting calls from the police, who were checking up to see how I was coping. I was delighted to be able to inform them of my visit to Tripoli and I told them that I would do everything in my power to persuade Fawzi to bring Nadia home.

During the wait, I had a visit from Bill, one of the parents at the nursery. Nadia was incredibly popular at nursery – everyone loved her and they often referred to her as 'their little star'. Bill was completely shocked and he told me that everyone there missed Nadia and hoped she would soon be back with her family and friends, where she belonged. No other parents contacted me – not because they didn't care about us but I think they really didn't know what to say. Bill assured me that all the parents were thinking about me and, if I needed anything, I could contact any one of them. The head of the nursery also came to visit me around the same time. She told me that they had Nadia's file at the nursery, which included copies of her drawings and various things. When I felt up to it, I could collect it or, if I preferred, she could drop it off. I agreed to go and get it as I felt it was important to show my face and tell everyone what was going on.

Nadia's file contained all the paintings that she had done, the first time she tried to write her name, the date she used the toilet by herself, her first hand and foot print. Every landmark and significant thing that she had achieved at nursery had all been recorded. She'd grown up so fast, and when I looked through all the paperwork I became very tearful. *This is all I have left of her*, I thought.

Bill had been doing some research on my behalf and he told me that he had read about a woman in a similar situation, whose children had been snatched by her husband and taken to Iraq. Apparently, she had taken a flight out there and snatched her children back. She had also written a book in which she related her tales of derring-do in rescuing children from all over the world. I was curious to know more, so Bill did an internet search. A few days later, he gave me a number to contact her. I was feeling nervous now because I hadn't thought of this as a possibility. *Was I heading in a different, more dangerous direction? What would happen if it all went wrong? I could lose Nadia forever.*

Anyway, I decided to phone this woman, Donya Al-Nahi, and we were on the phone for what seemed like hours! At last, I was speaking with someone who knew exactly what I had gone through and how I was feeling. I was in floods of tears as I went over everything – explaining my loss, telling her how empty I felt without my best friend, my daughter, my little bundle of joy. I told Donya that my heart bled for Nadia, and I was at a loss to know how to put things right.

Donya agreed to meet me but I would have to travel to London to see her. My brother Andrew volunteered to drive us there, but the traffic was terrible and we got lost on the way. We were being delayed and delayed, and I was afraid I would miss my appointment with Donya at our pre-arranged venue – a coffee shop in London's West End. Andrew then suggested it would be quicker if I took the train from Milton Keynes into the capital and he would follow on. By the time I reached London, I was pretty flustered.

As soon as I met Donya, I dissolved into tears of relief at her understanding manner. We exchanged stories and she told me exactly how she got her children back. *This woman's got balls*, I thought, as she explained how she had to do everything by herself. Donya told me she knew someone with contacts in Libya, who might be able to help. I was listening intently, hanging onto her every word. She told me everything that she had done and, more importantly, talked about all the other children she had helped get back from overseas. Donya told me she had contacts who would go and find Nadia, and take pictures of her. All I needed to do was supply her with an address, or even the area where Fawzi lived. She lifted my spirits and I was beginning to feel confident that, with her help, I could make something happen.

I then discovered that there was something else she needed – £1,500 to be exact. It seemed all this assistance and support came at a price. She told me that the contacts who could help me would be risking their lives and that's why such a sum was required. When I was in Libya some years later, having lived there for two-and-a-half years, I realised that this was not the only way but, at the time, I knew no better.

In any case, I couldn't make quick decisions but she seemed such a lovely person, who had been in the same boat as me. She knew exactly how I was feeling and so far she seemed the best person to help. A few days later, having thought about little else, I contacted Donya again: I told her where I thought Nadia might be in Tripoli, and transferred £1,500 into her bank account.

Over the next six weeks, I spoke to Donya nearly every other day and, although she kept my spirits up with her positive attitude, she didn't seem to have any concrete information for me. She told me that her contacts hang around outside their suspects' houses while they pretend to be working and take pictures of the abducted children; these things can't be rushed. I was confident that something would turn up soon.

At this point, GMTV contacted me and asked if I would appear on the early-morning show because they wanted to cover Nadia's story. I agreed, and the television company paid for Mum, Dad and me to stay in a London hotel for the night. I was to be interviewed by Kate Garraway and John Stapleton; Marek from the ISS would also be present. Mum and Dad asked me if I was nervous and I can honestly say that I wasn't. With everything else going on around me, it was the least of my worries and I thought any publicity would help; I just needed to do what I had to do.

I remember, during the interview, seeing footage of Nadia playing happily – a film that I had provided for the show. Seeing her gorgeous, innocent little face brought all my sadness back and I had to stop myself from welling up on national television. I also remember Kate Garraway asking Marek the question I had posed to him a few weeks ago: 'How many children are brought back from these countries?'

Marek's reply was something like: 'Well, to be honest, it's very difficult to get your child back from these countries. That's why the International Social Services arrange visits every year – just so that there is some contact.'

Throughout the interview I just kept shaking my head, thinking, 'This isn't right,' but they didn't show me on camera looking upset. I was also thinking, 'Over my dead body will I leave Nadia in that country. *I'll* show him!' In fact, I remember telling Kate Garraway that the next time I would be sitting on that sofa it would be with Nadia: 'You watch!'

My brother and Kirsty were married on 29 June 2007. It was incredibly emotional for all sorts of reasons and some of them the wrong ones. Of course, it wasn't the wedding that the happy couple would have wished for: they desperately wanted to celebrate their happiness, but I know they found it hard to completely let go without their bridesmaid. Nadia would have looked like a princess that day. She should have been standing proudly in the beautiful dress Andy and Kirsty had bought for her, clutching her bouquet. That's the way we had all imagined it, but Nadia wasn't there. I broke down several times during the day – I really didn't want to spoil the wedding, but I felt too sad, too unhappy.

Finally, in July, the day I had been waiting for was fast approaching – the day I would fly to Libya to see Nadia. My mum had agreed to come with me as she didn't want me to be alone. I knew it was going to be hard on the family while we were away, and I hoped they would be strong for each other. We agreed to stay in touch while we were away. Steph gave me a photograph of herself and Jay to give to Nadia, hoping she would remember them, and wrote her a message on the back: 'We love you, Nadia, please don't forget us. We miss you so much and pray to God I will see you again one day.'

I had decided to take all my legal documents with me to Libya, including the court orders that Fawzi had broken in the UK and records of all the terrible things he had done. Everything that I thought was sufficient proof to show a lawyer over there that he wasn't a good person and anything that might go against him in court. I took pictures of him drinking alcohol because I thought it would be really good evidence (Muslims are not supposed to drink) – this would prove what a bad person he was! In retrospect, it was all a bit naïve but I knew very little then.

Mum and I said an emotional goodbye to Dad and the rest of the family before travelling down to London. We had planned to stay with Donya the night before my flight because that way we wouldn't need to get an early train into London or pay for an expensive hotel. I was looking forward to seeing Donya again and meeting her family. She made us a lovely dinner and we were up most of the night talking about Nadia and what Fawzi's attitude to me would be.

I was so excited – I was desperate to see Nadia; I was also desperate to try to work something out with Fawzi, who had agreed to two weeks of supervised access, but he refused to divulge Nadia's address. Finally, I went to sleep but not before I had decided on something: I was going to snatch Nadia back!

How could I possibly enjoy two weeks with my daughter, knowing that was all the time we would have together? What about the other fifty weeks in the year when I needed her? There was no way I would settle for just two weeks. Taking Nadia back home was the only thing to do: I would go to Libya on the pretext of a short visit and then, while there, I was going to snatch my beloved daughter back.

CHAPTER 4

A Fortnight in Tripoli

The following morning, Donya dropped us off at the airport. She wished us luck and I thanked her for all her support. Daunted but excited, we went through the automatic doors into the terminal and almost immediately I received a call from Marek of the ISS to tell us where to meet.

Five minutes later, we were standing at the check-in with several other mothers who had been on this fortnightly visit for a few years. They looked happy that they were going to see their children, but there was also sadness in their faces that it was to be for only a short time.

Andrea was from France, Tracey hailed from London and amazingly Patricia only lived about five miles from me. I couldn't believe the coincidence and was thankful to discover that Fawzi wasn't the father of her child, too! Another woman, Anita, had had five of her children snatched. I wondered how on earth her ex-husband had managed to get all five out of the country without being caught. I knew how it felt to have one child taken, but I couldn't comprehend what Anita must have been going through. Terrifying.

Finally, it was time to board the plane. We went through security and Immigration then settled down in our seats. Mum has always been my rock and I was so pleased to have her with me. I was nervous, terrified and excited but there I was on 27 July 2007, two months to the day after Nadia was taken, on an aeroplane heading for Tripoli, the capital of Libya.

When we got off the plane, the first thing that hit me was the heat. I'd never felt heat like that before, it took my breath away. I couldn't breathe, but maybe this was because I was thinking about my baby. *How was she coping?* I was so close to her, yet she was still so far away. For a brief moment, I wondered if Fawzi would be there at the airport with Nadia but then I came to my senses. Of course he wouldn't be there. No way! *He will make me pay now*, I thought. *I'm in his country and he will make me suffer, big time.*

I noticed instantly that nearly everyone I saw was male. There was the occasional woman, but all the shops in the airport were run by men. It was clear from my first few minutes in Libya that the men here definitely dominate. I knew then that I was in for a tough battle. *Well, bring it on!*

We all boarded a minibus and were driven to a hotel complex, a tourist village called Janzour. It was like a UK Butlins holiday camp, but with not much to do. There were two swimming pools, a small arcade and a couple of bowling alleys, as well as a few shops that sold seaside bits and pieces. The complex was by the sea, so that was nice, but I wasn't really interested in the surroundings: I was just eager to see Nadia. It was about 3pm when we arrived. We were told to hand our passports in, and we were then given a key to our room. Usually, when I go abroad on holiday, I'm really excited to see my room. I'm always the first one to explore the living area, but this time I felt like I was in a daze. I had just two weeks and I thought I'd probably spend most of that time trying to persuade Fawzi to let me see Nadia.

After we'd been shown our rooms, Marek approached us and informed me that he would try to call Fawzi later. I was immediately annoyed.

'*Later*? Later is no good!' I told him. 'What about now?'

'Fawzi will be sleeping now, it's siesta time.'

I told Marek that I didn't care about Fawzi losing sleep – I'd lost enough sleep over the last two months: 'I don't care. Wake him up!'

Marek explained that he'd do his best so we decided to get something to eat and sat ourselves down in one of the small restaurants in the complex. I chose chicken and rice from the menu, and it actually tasted really nice. I must have eaten the same dish for the whole two weeks and I really got to like it! Funnily enough, I do miss it to this day. I had fruit for dessert, too. In fact, it was always fruit for dessert – I didn't eat a lot and I kept my meals simple because I was far too anxious to eat but I knew I had to eat something to keep my energy levels up.

Mum and I met up with the other mothers but we decided that we would try to keep ourselves to ourselves – I was finding it difficult to communicate and feeling quite anxious. I was here to see Nadia and I didn't want anyone messing with my head, dashing my hopes and telling me that I wouldn't get her back. I didn't want to hear anything negative – I was here to bring my daughter home, and that was that.

We had a walk around after lunch, but the heat was unbearable so we decided to go back to the hotel. I then saw Marek again. He had left a message for Fawzi but hadn't heard back. I asked Marek to find me a lawyer – I wanted some legal advice about my rights. He agreed to find someone for me and said he would arrange a meeting. He advised me to stay calm and said he would try to call Fawzi again later.

About 10.30pm that evening, Marek finally got back to me and informed me that Fawzi was on his way and would meet us in the hotel reception in half an hour. Mum and I went straight to reception, where we waited on tenterhooks. Fawzi arrived with his brother, Hamdi, but there was no sign of Nadia.

I asked him where Nadia was, to which he replied: 'Home.' I just wanted to hit him and shout, 'No, Nadia isn't at home, home is England!' So we talked for a while, trying to convince him to bring Nadia to me so that I could see her, but it was without success.

We enlisted the help of a Libyan called Muftah El Fagi, who Marek had introduced us to when we first arrived. Muftah worked for Watasimo, a charitable foundation run by Ayesha, the late Colonel Gaddafi's daughter. The charity provides financial assistance for British mothers to visit their children in Libya.

Muftah spoke English and his job was to negotiate with the Libyan fathers as to visiting rights. He and I tried for about two hours to negotiate with Fawzi. Although I begged Fawzi to let me see Nadia, I could tell that he loved having power over me. I would have done anything – *anything* – to see my daughter again. If he'd asked me, I would even have kissed his feet.

Fawzi finally agreed to my pleading and another of his brothers went to collect Nadia from where she was staying. He lived about forty-five minutes away from the complex so I had another couple of hours to wait. I kept thinking how tired Nadia would be – it was nearly midnight. In Libya, people kept very different hours. Often they would stay up all hours and only go to bed in the early hours of the morning, but this was no way to bring up a child. About an hour and half later, Fawzi went to check if they had arrived. Mum and I were sitting upstairs in the reception area when I heard Fawzi speak to someone. I couldn't understand what he was saying, but it was Nadia!

Fawzi brought her in. The moment I saw my baby, I burst into tears. Nadia looked bewildered and surprised, and I was so overwhelmed. Then her face broke into a huge smile as I ran to her and swept her up. Ecstatic, I threw my arms around her. I was sobbing uncontrollably and Mum came over and held us tight. I tried so hard not to make a big scene as I didn't want to upset Nadia, but I couldn't help it. Mum later told me that Fawzi couldn't bear to look at us; he turned away and his brother simply shook his head.

After two months, it was such a joy and relief to see Nadia again. *She was there; she was really there!* She was wearing black leggings and a black sleeveless top and sandals. Her nails were painted with Henna and her ears had been pierced. It was obvious that Fawzi was trying to show me that he was now very much in charge. He knew that I didn't like young children in black – I always think bright colours are much more fun. I also had told him on many occasions that I thought children should be old enough to decide for themselves if they want their body pierced. Fawzi had had Nadia's ears pierced just a few days before our arrival and she told me they were sore. It had become a power struggle and Fawzi was using Nadia to upset me.

Nadia became upset but Fawzi said that she had just woken up and was tired. *Nothing to do with her being kidnapped, taken to a foreign country and deprived of seeing her mother until now, of course not!* To keep the peace for the time being, I went along with what he was saying, though.

Fawzi then told me he had arranged to go and meet his mum and family at a nearby café with Nadia and me. I couldn't believe that he expected me to do this after all they had put me through. We reluctantly agreed to go, so we told Marek and Muftah where we were going and said we would be back in an hour.

Fawzi drove us there and Mum and I sat in the back of the car, holding Nadia as tight as we could. She rested her head on my chest and sobbed silently. Tears were running down her face uncontrollably. I tried to pull her away and asked what the matter was, but she refused to show me her face. Fawzi heard me ask her what was wrong and angrily, in Arabic, must have told Nadia to shut up. He repeated that she was tired. I was so upset – it was as if Nadia wasn't allowed to get upset about her mummy and, if ever she did, he would just tell her to shut up. Perhaps she was afraid to cry on occasions. I felt so sorry for her – I wanted to kill him. *How dare he put his own daughter through this? What must have been going through her little head?* She was far too young to be dealing with all this. *Nadia was just four years old, for God's sake – she was a baby and she needed me!*

We arrived at the café, and sat waiting was his family, huddled round in a circle, all smiles as if they'd done nothing wrong. Fawzi was throwing his weight about. I realised afterwards that in Libya men are considered superior to women – women do as they're told; even Fawzi's mum would do as he said. I used to wonder if his sisters and mother agreed with what he had done. *Didn't they have hearts, like Fawzi?* It seemed even if they disagreed with what he had done, they wouldn't say.

I used to wonder what he had told his family about me. Fawzi got into a lot of trouble in the UK, but I bet they didn't know anything about it. I'm sure he also hadn't told them that he was over £200,000 in debt back home. He probably misled the family by telling them that it was me who was in debt, and I was the one having affairs, just to turn them against me. There wasn't much conversation as none of his family spoke English, just lots of glances my way. His sister and mother would call Nadia and ask her to give them a hug. I hated them. *I hadn't seen my own daughter for two months and I had to watch them when all I wanted to do was grab Nadia's hand and run!* Poor Mum could see the hatred on my face, and the more they called Nadia and spoke to her in Arabic, the worse I was feeling.

After two hours of this purgatory, we made our way back to Janzour. It was now the middle of the night so Fawzi agreed to let Nadia sleep with me for the night, but it was also agreed that he would check into the room directly opposite us. We called Dad when we got back to the room and he spoke to Nadia lovingly, calling her 'my little chicken butty'. I knew that, as soon as he put the telephone down, he would start sobbing – he missed her so much. That night, I held her close and watched her sleep, as tears rolled down my face.

After my first night with Nadia, I kept a diary during the time I spent in Libya with Mum. I've decided to share these entries so people can really understand the hell I was going through, and just what stress Fawzi was putting us under.

29 July 2007

Didn't sleep much last night but my daughter was near me, so I was okay. I am really concerned for Nadia now, as she hasn't eaten properly all day – she just seems to pick at her food and she's withdrawn. Fawzi has got a room at the complex, just to keep an eye on us. He has met with another father who abducted his children over seven years ago, and I feel that he is having an influence on Fawzi and telling him what to do.

Spoke to Marek about all of my concerns. He is going to sit down with Nadia in a couple of days and try and get to know her a little better. Mum is being strong for the both of us. Marek has suggested Nadia may have to see a child psychologist. I know Fawzi has a big influence on her because she does all she can to please him, poor little thing. It's too much to deal with at such a young age. It must be hard for Nadia as she wants her mummy and daddy to be happy. I can't believe she has all this to deal with. I just hope Fawzi can see just how Nadia is with me and comes to his senses. I feel so guilty. It's my job to protect my daughter and I know what's best for my little girl, no one else. It's breaking my heart seeing her like this. I just want to tell her everything will be okay, but I can't. I can't make promises to her – I just want to take her home. Fawzi followed us everywhere we went today and wouldn't let us out of his sight.

30 July 2007

Got up late today. When we opened the door to leave the room, Fawzi was outside as if he had been waiting there all night, watching and making sure that we don't do a runner. Mum went for a walk earlier, around 8.30am, and she said he was there then. How am I supposed to enjoy time with my daughter when I have him watching me 24/7? He is watching our every move. Fawzi took us to a place that Nadia likes to call 'Wacky Warehouse'. It's a big indoor playground, with lots of slides, climbing frames, etc. I asked Fawzi if he didn't mind us being in Tripoli. He said he didn't, but he also said it wasn't the right time to talk. He wants me to feel it's like a holiday. He said we will discuss things two days before I leave – I'm not sure I can wait that long.

31 July 2007

Spoke to Theresa, one of the other mums, who's

been coming to Libya for seventeen years to see her son and daughter. She told me that Nadia will need a Libyan passport to get out of the country: although Nadia was born in the UK, apparently when a child with a Libyan father enters Libya, he or she is immediately classed as a Libyan national.

Neither Muftah nor Marek have informed me of this and they both know Fawzi will only let me know sometime later about whether he will let Nadia come home with me. I feel that all Marek and Muftah are bothered about is their little organisation, not concerned about getting my daughter back home. Theresa also informed me that, if I was to stay in Libya, Fawzi would have to provide for us both.

Went to the Roman museum today and a camera crew came along. The filming is only for the charity and not for a TV broadcast. I feel like I'm being watched. I told Muftah that, if Fawzi won't let Nadia come home, then I'm staying here. If Fawzi is only going to agree to me taking her home two days before we leave, we won't have enough time to sort out the visas.

Marek came to see me after I had spoken to Muftah and told me they are doing everything they can to help me. My case has gone to 'the high board' and maybe in two or three days the head of the charity and Ayesha Gaddafi will come here to speak to me.

When we arrived back from the playground, I

noticed Fawzi was talking with a Muslim woman. She was constantly watching me, and I saw Fawzi slide some money over to her. She refused but he obviously said, 'Take it!' He walked her to the main entrance and outside the gates and then, ten minutes later, he came back and told me that the woman was from a children's magazine. I didn't know what he was talking about, but he wouldn't say any more.

Fawzi invited us to his house this evening. Mum was suspicious and so I telephoned Donya in England, who advised us to go. Fawzi's family made us feel very welcome and his mum seemed very pleased to see me. She kept hugging and kissing me – perhaps she's afraid that I'm going to take her granddaughter back to England. I felt like they were putting on a big effort to prove to me that Nadia is being properly looked after. I could tell that Nadia didn't really want to be there and she was very clingy towards me and upset, although she settled down after a while. I noticed if any of the other children present were getting attention, Nadia would become jealous. It made me realise that they are all doing what they can to make Nadia feel like this is her home. It's like they are bribing her and giving everything she asks for.

1 August 2007

Nothing much happened today. Got up late again – I think it's all the hot weather making us sleepy. We went swimming. Fawzi was around all the time. After a while I took Nadia for a shower, Mum stayed with Fawzi, and afterwards we all went for lunch. Fawzi is still acting very nice to me, but I'm concerned as I don't know how he will react at the end of the week. Is this a big game he's playing? Is he going to tear my heart into pieces? We still haven't received our passports back from reception.

That night I got Nadia to speak to Steph back home. I knew Steph was upset at hearing Nadia's voice, but she tried to stay calm and strong for us. Steph must have wanted to hold Nadia in her arms so much.

2 August 2007

Quiet day today. Stayed in the complex. We took a stroll to the main entrance of the complex to see if it would be easy to get out. It was, and we came back in through another entrance. The guards demanded ID and asked if we were staying at the complex, which made me realise they didn't know who we were. Our plan to snatch Nadia could work, if only we had our passports. Took Nadia swimming. Fawzi was around the whole time. We went for something to eat and Fawzi turned up halfway through, sitting with a couple of guys who work here, and kept asking Nadia to go over to them to show her off. We met Fawzi again at 8pm and, after waiting around an hour-and-a-half, he said he would take us into Tripoli.

Fawzi arrived at 8pm and, sort of out of the blue, Nadia asked, 'Can I go to England, Baba?' ('Baba' is Arabic for 'Daddy'.)

'No,' he said.

I asked him why.

'She will never go to England again,' he told me.

It was like a sword through my heart. I asked, 'How can you live with that, knowing you've taken your daughter away from her mummy?' He just shrugged his shoulders. I followed this up: 'Do your family know what you've done?'

He said yes, but I could tell he was lying as he was very sheepish and it was clear that he was hiding something.

I told Fawzi that I would fight him for Nadia. He just repeated that Nadia wasn't going back to England. I told him to leave us alone and I walked away. Maybe I shouldn't have done that but I might have said something I would have regretted. All the time I was being reasonable to him because I didn't want to upset Nadia, or give him an excuse to take her back to his home, where I wouldn't get to see her.

I hated him more than ever now.

I went to see Marek and told him what had just happened. He sympathised with me, and said he would have a private talk tomorrow. I told him that we had been there for six days now and nothing had been done in legal terms. I'd not been given any advice. I stressed that I was prepared to stay for as long as it takes to sort things out and that my dad was going to send me some money so we could stay longer. I also told him that I wanted my passport back.

Nadia told me several times that she wanted to go to England and asked why her daddy wouldn't let her. Marek could see Nadia was upset and she started crying again. She doesn't want to be here, and I can't do anything to help her.

I'm powerless – I hate it here, I hate Fawzi.

3 August 2007

Fawzi was very standoffish with me this morning. I apologised for what I said yesterday, although I meant every word. I tried to act normal and asked him if we were going to see his family today. He said he would let me know later. Fawzi is still mixing with one of the other dads. The other dad's ex-wife, Anita, told me she is suspected of being a member of al-Qaeda and was wanted by INTERPOL for kidnapping. I can't believe he's able to walk about as though he owns the place and he doesn't allow his children to go out with their mother. I'm worried that he will have an influence on Fawzi's decisions.

Fawzi's family arrived and he completely changed. He was like a different person, all nice again. I'm sure his family don't know what he's done by snatching Nadia. I think he may have told them that I voluntarily allowed her to come to Libya, or that

I'm some sort of drug addict. I still haven't spoken to Marek, hopefully later tomorrow.

4 August 2007

A trip to another museum was planned for today at 10am. We had breakfast and were on the bus outside reception for 9.30am. Anita's ex-husband, Ezzideen, was there, guarding the bus, making sure none of his children boarded. A few minutes later, Fawzi arrived. Ezzideen obviously called him, so he also came to check on us. These fathers make our visits so uncomfortable; how are we supposed to enjoy our time with our children when we are watched over all the time?

Everywhere we go, Fawzi is always right behind us. I can't breathe without him being there and watching over us. Nadia seems to be coming round now, she seems to be eating more, although I can see that she has changed since being here. She sulks every time I say no to her. Fawzi bribes her all the time. He says things like: 'I'll let you sleep with Mummy if you give me a kiss.' This is no way to bring up a child – I will not allow this to happen. I hate the bastard: the more I see him, the more I despise him. I have to pretend to be nice to him when all I want to do is smack him very hard.

I really feel for Anita – she has five children that she comes to visit every year in this shit hole. Her husband doesn't allow her to go on any trips, or even out of the complex. Anita does this every year – I really don't know how she copes – and there's not much to do, as it's not exactly The Ritz.

Managed to speak to Marek; told him the whole story and how Fawzi really doesn't have any interest in Nadia. Marek listened, but didn't comment. He told me he is going to the main office of the charity tomorrow morning, and he will get back to me later. We've been here a week now and still nothing has been done to assist me getting my child back to the country she was born in. No one is helping me, not even our government. I can't believe that these people are allowing this to happen when kids go missing every year – it's like they are condoning what these bastards have done by letting them get away with it.

I will never give up on my daughter; I love her so much it hurts.

Apart from this morning, we didn't see much of Fawzi and stayed out of his way. He must be thinking that I'm up to something.

Mum is desperate to speak to my dad but the phone lines have been down. She wants to see how he is and hear about Steph, Andrew and Kirsty. I know she is torn about being away from Dad and staying with me, but I really need her here. She is my rock.

5 August 2007

Went for breakfast and met another mother. Her

name is Sharon. Her child was taken to Benghazi. She has had to pay for all her own accommodation here in the hotel and her flight to Benghazi. That doesn't seem fair. All our flights and accommodation were paid for by the ISS. I thought this charity paid for all of us mums to come here. Why was it different for Sharon?

When I saw Marek and Muftah I had a real go at them, telling them that I've been here over a week and I have had no answers. I want to know what my rights are, and I asked them about my legal position. Muftah came up with some bullshit about waiting a couple of days. I'd been told to wait a couple of days when we first got here and I need to extend my visa if I want to stay. I told both of them that no one can help in England, and no one is helping here.

Marek came to my room later and said he was going to see a solicitor tomorrow. I said I'd go with him, but he told me he wanted to speak to them on his own first. That probably means it's all a load of nonsense. The other mums and I have decided to hold a meeting with Marek and Muftah tomorrow to find out what exactly is going on. I should have seen a solicitor as soon as I arrived, not a week into the visit.

6 August 2007

A bad day today. At the meeting with Marek and Muftah, all the mothers were asking them what exactly their job entails and how are they supposed to be helping us. Neither of them could answer our questions and we all got upset. Marek told me that we now don't have enough time to sort a solicitor out. I asked him when would be the right time and why hadn't he told me yesterday. I feel I'm being fobbed off and that it's Fawzi who is being protected. Towards the end of the meeting, Fawzi walked past with his brother, saying he wanted to see Nadia. Marek told Fawzi that this was a private meeting and they should leave. They looked angry, but went away.

Later in the day, I went to try and get my passport. I was getting desperate, and in any case I needed my passport to change money. An hour later Fawzi approached me: 'What do you want your passport for?' It's incredible – he seems to have everyone watching us.

Tonight Fawzi has demanded Nadia stay with him, in his room opposite. He frogmarched her back and there was nothing I could do about it. Nadia was weeping quietly again because she isn't allowed to cry properly in front of him. She didn't want to go with him, she wanted to stay with me and she can see exactly what he's doing because she's a bright little thing. He's punishing her as well as me, and it hurts me so much to see this.

7 August 2007

Didn't sleep well last night. I keep going over in my

head when I have to say goodbye to Nadia. I feel sick constantly. I can't enjoy myself here, and my little girl will feel the same when I have to go home. I'm not eating again – I just want to go home now with Nadia. He doesn't understand how much it's affecting her. Can't the ISS see that they are protecting him?

Mum finally managed to speak to Dad. She said he sounded really down and is missing and worrying about us.

8 August 2007

Got up today, not really knowing what to expect from Fawzi. Mum had a quiet word with him and thanked him for letting us come here and spend time with Nadia. She felt that he listened and acknowledged what she was saying. She explained that she and Dad have supported him in the past and would still support him back in England. He nodded. Mum talked a lot about England to him and what we used to do. He said that I should listen to Mum and Dad more, and not to my friends. Not sure what he meant by this. Mum started to cry and asked Fawzi why he wouldn't come home. He said he'd talk to me in a couple of days. I suppose there's still a little hope.

We went swimming afterwards and Fawzi joined us. He pretended to push me into the water, and he put his arms around me as if to hug me. Perhaps that's a good sign? I would never have Fawzi back, but if I have to play the doting wife to get him to come home, then I'll do it. Whatever it takes.

We arranged to go shopping this evening and, while we were having dinner out in Tripoli, a young boy made some remark about me. Fawzi reacted angrily and shouted something to him in Arabic.

9 August 2007

Got up today feeling depressed. I'm tired and stressed – today's the day when Fawzi wants to talk to me. We went into Tripoli first and bought a couple of bracelets and earrings. I mentioned to him that we are meant to be having 'that chat' today and he agreed we would once we were back at the complex and once he's had something to eat and showered. He's messing me about, playing with my emotions. I'm so anxious, I feel sick with fear.

Fawzi called me and we met at the coffee shop. I started the talking and suggested that, if he comes back to England, we could sort things out. He replied that if he came back to England he would be in trouble with the police because of the kidnap. I told him, if he brought Nadia back, I would arrange for the charges to be dropped. I never mentioned to him that, if he did set foot in England, he might get arrested on the deception charges.

Fawzi said that he needed proof that all charges were to be dropped and if he had proof then he would allow Nadia to come home. I didn't believe him for one second. In my heart of hearts I know he won't let Nadia come home and he's waited all this time to tell me as he knows it's too late for me to sort something out to stay. The bastard!

He has even told Nadia that there will be lots of presents waiting for her when she goes back to the family house, just so she won't want to come back with me. How can he treat his four-year-old daughter like this?

I had a meeting today with Marek and the British Ambassador, Vincent Fean, who was very nice and sympathetic but couldn't offer any concrete solutions. I'm too distraught to think, sleep or eat. A meal and bowling was planned this evening for the mothers and their children. Halfway through dinner, all the fathers turned up and sat at a table opposite ours. Anita was fuming. She was shouting at the top of her voice, making sure everyone could hear how angry she was. Her ex approached our table and instructed her to move tables because she was at the same table as Marek and Muftah – both men! Is he for real? The whole thing is a joke. All we ask is for two weeks' hassle-free time with our children. I hate this place and I hate Anita's ex. He is definitely having an influence on Fawzi.

Fawzi mentioned yesterday about going to his mum's for a meal before we go home. Is he having a laugh? There's no way I'm going there; it would be like accepting what he's done and accepting that it's okay for Nadia to stay. There's no way I'm playing 'happy families' any more. There are just one-and-a-half days until we say, 'See you soon,' to Nadia because I *will* see her soon. I'm not going to say goodbye to her as that sounds like it's final, like I won't see her again. How do I explain to a four-year-old that her mummy is going home and I can't take her with me?

10 August 2007

We got up late today and Nadia heard Mum tell the cleaner that we are going home tomorrow. Nadia became very upset again and told me she doesn't want me to go home unless she can come with me. I received a call from Fawzi on my mobile, asking what we were doing. Maybe he's getting nervous now. If he doesn't see us around the complex, he's calling me, checking up on me to see if I'm still here. I told him we were going swimming. We hadn't been in the pool for five minutes before one of his brothers turned up to keep us under surveillance.

About ten minutes later, he phoned Fawzi on his mobile and, not long after that call, Fawzi turned up. He was messing around with Nadia for a while, until he plucked up the courage to come over and ask if we were still going to his mum's today. I replied, 'Under the circumstances, I'm not going. I want to spend time with Nadia.' As soon as I said this, he walked away, ignoring Nadia.

Mum, Nadia and I went down for coffee. Fawzi turned up and said his mum was coming over this evening to visit us. After dinner, he turned up with his mum and six of his family members. I hugged and kissed them all for Nadia's sake, of course. I felt that if I was rude towards any of his family, or to him, then he would stop all contact completely. I hated all of them for allowing this to happen but again I had to put on a brave face. I started to cry. I was curious to know what they must have been thinking. I know Nadia won't be looked after by her father here, she will be passed on to the mother or sister, or even some other relative.

Fawzi repeated that as soon as I send over the documentation to prove that I've dropped the charges he will come back with Nadia. Now I'm confused and don't know what he will do.

Perhaps there's a chance…

11 August 2007

Very emotional day today; woke Nadia up to tell her Mummy's leaving today. It's the hardest thing I have ever had to say and I've been putting it off for days. She woke in tears, asking me not to leave and said that she wants to come with me. She begged me not to go, my heart was breaking all over again – how could he do this to us?

Everyone is feeling tense, upset – no one knows what to say to each other. This last fortnight Mum has been my rock, and I couldn't have done this without her. It just shows how much a daughter needs her mum. All the mothers are 'here for each other' and promised to keep in touch.

I explained to Nadia that she will be in England sometime and that's what her daddy's promised her, but it still didn't help much. We packed all her things together, as well as her old toys that we brought with us, and then walked over to Fawzi's room. Nadia was holding Mum's and my hand tightly, and I promised her that I would see her soon, no matter what.

Mum and I arrived at his room feeling helpless. I sat Nadia down, told her I had to leave now and that I would be back soon. I felt so helpless and tried to hold back the tears but couldn't help myself. Nadia was screaming, 'Daddy, Daddy, I want my mummy!' Mum and I also started shouting, 'Please, please, Fawzi, let her come home!' He wouldn't listen. I got up to leave and Nadia was still screaming for me. I asked Fawzi to do one last thing for me: 'Please, please, I beg of you, please don't let Nadia see me leave in the bus!'

The last thing I said to Nadia was to be brave. How could this low-life bastard put us both through this? How could he sit there and see how upset we both are and show no emotion? He doesn't care for Nadia, I can see that so clearly now. As I closed the door to leave Nadia was in tears, but she said to me, 'I'll be brave, Mummy.' It was like a knife through my heart – I just wanted to take her in my arms and run.

Mum was in tears the whole time, too. She's been so strong for me, while I was a total wreck. The journey to the airport on the bus was silent. This isn't right. All of us mothers were in tears; we didn't know what to say to each other. What must Nadia think of me? I cannot do anything in my power to help her. I've had to hand Nadia back. She was crying and it broke my heart to have to let her go back to Fawzi. I couldn't bear to go home without her, but I was completely helpless.

There was nothing I could do.

CHAPTER 5

Righting the Unrightable Wrong

The four-hour flight home from Tripoli was truly awful. Most of the mothers were crying and the atmosphere on the plane was miserable. There were some other passengers – mainly Libyan – unconnected with our party, who were surprisingly unaware of what was going on with us. One of the stewardesses asked why we were so sad, and when we told her she brought us all champagne. It was a lovely goodwill gesture and made me think there were some kind people around.

Later on, I started to contemplate the situation and began feeling a bit more positive. It must have been the champagne! When I'd left Fawzi, it had been made quite clear that, if I dropped the charges regarding the abduction, he would bring Nadia home. That's what I had to focus on. I now had to decide how I was going to play this: should I go public again and make everyone aware of what I was doing, or keep quiet and deal with things my way? I thought that if I went to the media it would show Fawzi how serious I was about getting Nadia home, but, on the other hand, it might make him run and hide.

Mum was being as strong as ever and doing her best to console me, but I was heartbroken and wondered when I would next see Nadia. I knew that she was happy for me, that I had been able to spend two weeks with Nadia, laughing and giggling together like old times, but I also realised that she was inconsolable because we had left Libya without her granddaughter. We were both looking forward to seeing Dad, but knew that he would be upset that Nadia wasn't on the plane with us.

When we landed at Heathrow, Dad was at the airport, waiting for us. As soon as I saw him, I rushed to him and fell into his arms like I was a little girl again. I started crying and, in between sobs and gasping for air, I spluttered: 'I tried, I tried so hard, Dad, but he wouldn't let her come with me! I tried, Dad, I did my best...' Dad cuddled me and tried to make me feel better. When I had composed myself a little, I told him, 'All I can do now is drop these charges and hope Fawzi sticks to his word and brings Nadia home.'

Donya and her husband had also come to the airport to greet us. Later, we all had a drink in a café near their house, and I asked her what I should do. I told Donya exactly how Fawzi had behaved and asked if she had any idea what might be going on in his head. I had spent the last two weeks trying to work this out for myself, but I was emotionally drained. Donya was optimistic and said, 'Let's see if he sticks to his word.' The first thing I had to do was to make sure that the charges were dropped and then decide what my next move should be.

Steph and Andrew met us at Wigan station and accompanied us back to the house. They had been hoping and praying that Nadia would be with us and it tore them apart when they realised Mum and I had come home alone. All the family spent the evening together and we filled in the others about the details of our trip. We had taken lots of photographs of Nadia, which they devoured.

On our return, I discovered that there were an incredible number of good-luck cards waiting for me. I realised so many people were giving me lots of support and it made me even more determined to get Nadia back, no matter what the cost. I told everyone that we had to remain positive and hopeful; being negative wasn't an option. Having said that, waking up in Wigan without Nadia's arms wrapped around me on that first morning was heart-wrenching. I had just been getting used to cuddling her, feeling the warmth of her body next to mine at night-time and bonding with her again and now it had all been taken away. But I had to be strong, to be focused: so long as I kept up the momentum and kept myself occupied, I'd be okay.

The first thing I did was to telephone Fawzi and ask if

I could speak to Nadia. He passed the phone to her without a word, and she said to me, 'Am I going to England tomorrow, Mummy?'

'In a few days' time, darling,' I replied.

'After I've been to nursery, I'll come to England, Mummy,' Nadia continued. But then the line went dead.

It was lovely to hear her voice again and surprisingly this very short conversation gave me some hope; Fawzi must be telling her that she is going to come back to us, maybe it could happen. I just hoped that he would stick to his word.

Immediately I rang Wigan Police Station and spoke to a female detective constable called Lynne. I explained the whole situation to her and could tell that she was taken aback. She seemed a little uncertain – well, I suppose this was unusual and not many police officers would have come across cases of children being snatched by their dad and taken to Libya. However, she agreed to visit me at home.

What I didn't know at the time was that a man, who was to prove invaluable in the ordeal that I was to go through in the coming years, was in the room and was ear-wigging our conversation. Chief Inspector Phil Owen, who was based in Manchester but a crime manager in the Wigan Division, happened to be in the room. When Lynne came off the phone, he asked her what the call was about. She told him and, when he learned the seriousness of the situation, he suggested that he should accompany her. The situation had struck a personal chord: Phil had two daughters himself. He and Lynne arrived shortly afterwards and, from the beginning, I trusted him straight away. Calm and authoritative, he seemed to get a handle on the situation immediately.

I told them the whole story from start to finish. Phil was extremely sympathetic, but was totally honest with me from the beginning about how difficult this was going to be. I appreciated his openness; I didn't want any false hopes, I wanted to be told how it was. I convinced Phil that Fawzi wouldn't consider coming back to England unless the charges were dropped and that he would have to try to sort that out, otherwise there was no chance of getting Nadia back. Phil agreed that he would look into the matter straight away.

Meanwhile, I was still calling Nadia each day and I'd decided my best bet was to be friendly with Fawzi. I think it confused him a little that I was so calm; it probably made him feel that I was up to something, and I made sure that, every time we spoke, I would inform him of the progress of the court proceedings and that I expected the charges to be dropped at any time. I also listened very carefully to every word that he said to try to pick up any clues as to what he was really thinking or planning.

Speaking to Phil much later, I realised how much he had protected me. It was only when he started looking into the various procedures that he understood the enormity of the task. It was quite a tall order to get the kidnapping charges dropped and he quickly discovered that it didn't usually apply to this sort of situation. Such deals were usually only struck with criminal witnesses, who were willing to testify for the police and in return they would be given some sort of immunity against prosecution. Phil, however, was determined to succeed and took it upon himself as a personal, as well as professional, challenge. Later he admitted: 'I could see the sort of person I was dealing with, and knew that you would never let this go.' Early on, he had realised that I was completely fixated on getting the charges dropped and he was dead right!

The plan was to obtain a Certificate of Immunity, which had to be issued by the Director of Public Prosecutions (DPP), so Phil started negotiations with the local DPP in Manchester and then engaged in lengthy discussions with the London office. At the outset, he didn't even know how they could serve the certificate on Fawzi.

Phil made contact with the Child Abduction Centre through the British Foreign & Commonwealth Office, who were marvellous support and very helpful. He also liaised with the International Social Services, who provided a letter of support stating that Nadia needed two parents and that, if Fawzi should return to England with her and reconciliation with me was possible, it would not be in Nadia's best interests if her father was jailed.

Phil explained what had to be done, and we agreed that we should give Fawzi a time limit so that he didn't drag things out. I had some reservations as Fawzi didn't like to be told what to do or to be given ultimatums, but otherwise we might be waiting forever for a decision from him. Phil was brilliant and actually called round almost every other day and talked things through with me. He always lifted my spirits, although he never tried to bullshit me or give me false hope. I could rely on him 100 per cent. He was incredibly reassuring, both in his professional role and as a sympathetic man, and seemed to understand exactly what I was going through.

My dad had had a reasonable relationship with Fawzi when he had been in Wigan, and, coming from a patriarchal society, Fawzi seemed to respond to the person whom he considered to be the 'head of the household'. Dad had tried, through gritted teeth, to reason with Fawzi but to no avail.

Again, we turned to Phil for further help. He had been trained as a hostage negotiator and offered to talk to Fawzi and endeavour to get a feel of what he was thinking. I agreed as I thought it couldn't do any harm, and Phil certainly knew what he was doing (he has since become involved in negotiating other child-abduction cases). He discussed strategies of dealing with Fawzi with other hostage-negotiator colleagues before telephoning him then he tried to explain to Fawzi how unfair this was on Nadia, and how much a young child needs her mother. Phil also described how, if Fawzi did return, custody arrangements could be made so that he could have equal access to Nadia. But Fawzi just wasn't to be persuaded. I had even offered, totally insincerely, to give the marriage another go but Fawzi refused this peace offering, too.

Phil soon realised that it would take more than a few reasonable words to convince Fawzi. He tried again with a different tack, this time attempting to encourage him to come back with Nadia by telling him he wouldn't be arrested. Fawzi wanted reassurances about the kidnapping charge. Phil guaranteed – although at that time he didn't have the authority to offer this as a bargaining tool – that Fawzi wouldn't be in any trouble for any of his past misdemeanours; he would make sure of it. Unfortunately, Fawzi was his usual mealy-mouthed self and kept his cards close to his chest. His only response was: 'I'll think about it.'

After some weeks, thanks to Phil's determination and hard work, he had finally managed to convince the authorities not to prosecute Fawzi. The formalities had been completed and the Certificate of Immunity obtained through the legal process; the certificate only lasted fourteen days – the police didn't want the immunity to be open-ended, which would give Fawzi the opportunity to delay any decision. Officials of the British Embassy had agreed to give Fawzi the necessary paperwork and demonstrate that the legal process was totally legitimate. Phil had also discovered that the authorities couldn't touch Fawzi for the other charges due to insufficient evidence so, if he had returned to England, he would not be arrested.

Although this had all taken much longer than I'd

envisaged, I was naturally thrilled. I called Fawzi and told him that the kidnapping charges had been dropped. He sounded okay, even a little bit upbeat which pleased me, but he didn't really say very much other than he would look at the certificate.

I'd done everything that Fawzi had asked of me.

A few days later, the certificate had arrived in Libya, and I was told that Arvinder Vohra, the Vice Consul of the British Embassy, would be passing the paperwork to Fawzi during a meeting in four days' time. I couldn't believe it wasn't going to happen straight away, but yet again I had to be patient.

On the day that Arvinder was due to meet Fawzi, I was up very early and I sat by the phone most of the day. If I'm honest, I was hoping for Fawzi to receive the certificate and then tell me that he would be on the next flight home with Nadia. I played it over in my head numerous times, imagining meeting them at the airport and Nadia running into my arms. I even asked Phil if he could take me to the airport by helicopter – bit cheeky, I know!

Finally, I got the call to say that Arvinder had passed the documents on to Fawzi but I wanted more information. I wanted to know exactly how it happened; I needed to know exactly where it was (apparently a seedy café in Tripoli), what was said, and what was Fawzi's reaction. Was he relieved, even pleased? At least I knew that he had turned up and the papers were served.

I called Fawzi that evening. He informed me that he

had received the certificate but it was in English, so he had to have it translated. In the nicest possible way, I asked how long that would take. 'Soon' was all he said.

Well, a week passed by and I had heard nothing: Fawzi wasn't talking to me. I asked Phil if he could chase it up; I was now getting anxious.

Unfortunately, the next we heard was that Fawzi wasn't happy with the time limit and some of the wording on the certificate. Although devastated, I forced myself to remain focused and calm. I rang Fawzi and put it on speakerphone so that Phil could listen in. Phil felt Fawzi was playing for time; Ramadan was coming up and I knew that nothing would happen throughout this holy time, even though during this month of fasting all Muslims are supposed to do the right thing by God and make amends with family and friends.

This procedure had taken a lot of work, negotiation and time to achieve and now the whole process had to begin again, with the wording changed to accommodate Fawzi's concerns. When I heard the news I was devastated, and Phil Owen was none too happy about starting all over again.

Phil agreed to speak to Fawzi again to see if he could get more information out of him. Fawzi confirmed that he didn't want to be bothered during Ramadan and said he would make his decision after the next Islamic festival – Eid (a day of festivities which signifies the end of Ramadan). There was nothing I could do; I just had to wait for another month while the bastard made his mind up.

I decided to go back to work just for a short time until Ramadan was over. At this point I needed something to distract me – I'd been totally obsessed with fighting Fawzi and the situation had taken over my life to the detriment of everything else. I wasn't socialising and, although my family were incredibly supportive, there must have been times when they couldn't bear to hear me going on and on about it. We all needed a bit of a break, and I realised that I couldn't go on like this.

When I went back to work, my work colleagues were fantastic. They just let me get on with my job and do what I could. It was difficult for some of them because they didn't know what to say. I was quite open and I made it clear that I would rather have people come and ask me questions to my face and be direct than talk about me behind my back. Even so, naturally I couldn't shut off completely. Every day while at work I would take a five-minute break during which I would try to contact Fawzi. Most of the time he would be sleeping and wouldn't answer the phone. It seemed that, during Ramadan, he would sleep most of the day and be up most of the night. I knew Fawzi and had seen for myself what he's like when fasting. During this period, he would also stop smoking and he'd become very grumpy without his nicotine fix. I understood that I would have to tread carefully while the festival was on; I wouldn't want to upset him and so, yet again, much against my better nature I was holding back.

I started to call during the evenings to see if I could catch him then, which I did on a few occasions. While talking to him, I tried to keep upbeat and reiterated that he would be doing the right thing if he brought Nadia home. If I'm honest, I really played on the fact that it was Ramadan, when Muslims are supposed to be at their most religious and doing the right thing by Allah. I also spoke to Nadia every two or three days.

At the end of Eid, I steeled myself for the definitive answer. The Certificate of Immunity had been amended to Fawzi's satisfaction and he had no excuses left. I'd had enough by then and I was at my wits' end so I rang and asked him: 'When are you bringing Nadia home?'

Flatly and without emotion, he replied: 'I don't think I am coming home.'

It was now obvious to me that during this time he had been playing games and never had any intention of coming back with Nadia. I suppose, deep down, I had always thought this would be his response but I had to hang onto some hope.

I simply said, 'Okay.' I think he was surprised by my reaction. I'm sure he had expected me to become angry, but I was just too distraught to say any more. I hung up. Time to do things my way. I had nothing to lose – I didn't care if I never saw Fawzi again – all I wanted was my baby back.

There was also another episode, during this time, which gave us false hope: at one stage, Phil thought that they had actually persuaded Fawzi into agreeing to bring Nadia home. The outgoing Assistant British Ambassador to Libya, Robert Brown, offered to accompany Fawzi and

Nadia back to the UK and to go through Immigration and ensure he was not arrested as he entered Britain. According to Phil, Fawzi had agreed, but, just before the trip was about to take place, Brown was transferred to another post. Fawzi changed his mind and then went to the British Embassy and told them that he wasn't going to return, even if he was safeguarded against kidnapping charges. Phil came to tell me what had happened – I think he dreaded it because he knew what my reaction would be. Naturally, I was bitterly disappointed and I also realised this was my last chance. I knew then that Fawzi would never return to the UK and I had to take matters into my own hands.

I telephoned Donya immediately. She suggested I go and stay with her for a couple of days, to think things over and give myself a break. I thought it was a good idea and, a few days later, I took the train to London and found my way to her house. Donya immediately advised me to go to Libya. I told her I had no money – it would mean my selling everything I had – but, if that's what I had to do, then of course I would.

Donya informed me I would need a visa to enter Libya, but I shouldn't worry as she had contacts and could sort it out, although I would have to pay for the arrangements and obtain the visa. She told me that if I went to the visa office in London myself then I could be refused entry as the Libyan authorities might guess that I was going over there to snatch Nadia back. It made sense, so Mum, Dad and I took out a loan and paid Donya £3,000. This would also cover the cost of Donya's visit to Libya, as she had explained to me that, if we didn't get custody of Nadia, we would revert to our original plan, in which she was going to help me snatch Nadia. She was insistent that we had to keep our friendship quiet because of her reputation. As soon as people knew we were in cahoots, I might be refused entry into Libya. The more I talked about snatching Nadia back, the more I felt confident enough to do it.

I didn't know then how strict Libya was, but I realised that I had to be careful. Donya seemed to know what she was talking about, though, because she'd been through it all herself with her own children, so I had no reason to doubt her.

Just listening to Donya gave me confidence and it felt like I wasn't in it alone. She had promised to join me in a month's time. However, she did inform me that, as I was the mother of a missing child, my name would be known at Immigration at the Libyan borders and airports, which would make it difficult for me to get out of the country with Nadia. Donya said she knew how to sort this out, but it would cost me a further £3,000.

I agreed to pay. All I could think about was getting Nadia back and any price was worth paying. I knew Fawzi would make it as difficult as possible for me, and Libya was, after all, a very different country to ours. Anything that might help would be a sensible investment. So to have a friend in Donya, who helped women and who had experienced exactly what I was going through, was brilliant. I had no choice but to trust her.

Donya advised me to get a security guy at Tripoli Airport to look after me and help me through Immigration. Need I say any more? She could arrange this for a further £2,000. It all made sense – I had to make sure I was doing it right; I didn't want any trouble. Donya told me that she knew of a family in Libya with whom I could stay when I arrived and who would interpret for me and accompany me to the lawyer's. This was brilliant – I had no idea where I was going to stay otherwise. It was an incredibly kind offer from complete strangers.

I returned from London and sat down with the whole family and told them what I had decided to do: I was going to take leave from my job, sell my car and other possessions, take out a loan and put the money into moving to Libya. I was sure that I would only be there for a month and I'd be back before Christmas. Donya said she would come out to Libya after a month to meet me and Nadia and I'd be on my way home with Nadia soon afterwards. Mum and Steph started to cry, while Andy and Dad gave me huge hugs. Naturally, they were all very worried for me but not once, then or later, did they ever try to talk me out of it. They gave me total and unconditional support: the bottom line was they knew that I would never be able to live with myself if I didn't try everything in my power to make things right. As I promised to bring Nadia home, I asked them all to be strong for me.

My brother set up a website in an attempt to raise money towards my legal fees, with links to various charities and organisations that dealt with child abduction. Andy's wife, Kirsty, and two of our cousins, Lee and Simon Scofield, as well as a work colleague of Dad's, all did parachute jumps for the charity.

I now had to decide whether to try to sort this out on my own without media involvement. Having the press on board might upset the Libyan authorities, but, after much thought, I decided the publicity would probably serve me best in making the situation known to as many people as possible. In any case, it was also possible that some members of the media might find out what was going on.

I'd already received some coverage in the local press when I arrived home from my two-week visit in the summer so I contacted the *Wigan Echo* again when I decided to give everything up to go to Libya. I also spoke on BBC Radio and Granada, and appeared on Sky television to publicise the fact that I'd done all I could in the UK. Only one more option remained to get Nadia back: I had to return to Libya.

During this time, I received an email via my brother's website from a lady called Fiona. She claimed to be living in Tripoli and said she knew where Nadia was. Apparently, she had seen Nadia and said she was doing fine. Fiona added: 'Nadia is well looked after and seems to be happy.' She also mentioned that her friend's son attended the same school as Nadia. Although partly relieved, I was doubtful as to the sincerity of such a message. Was this someone trying to find out information on Fawzi's behalf,

precious daughter Nadia was a ‘miracle’ baby. She is my life, and I will anything to protect her.

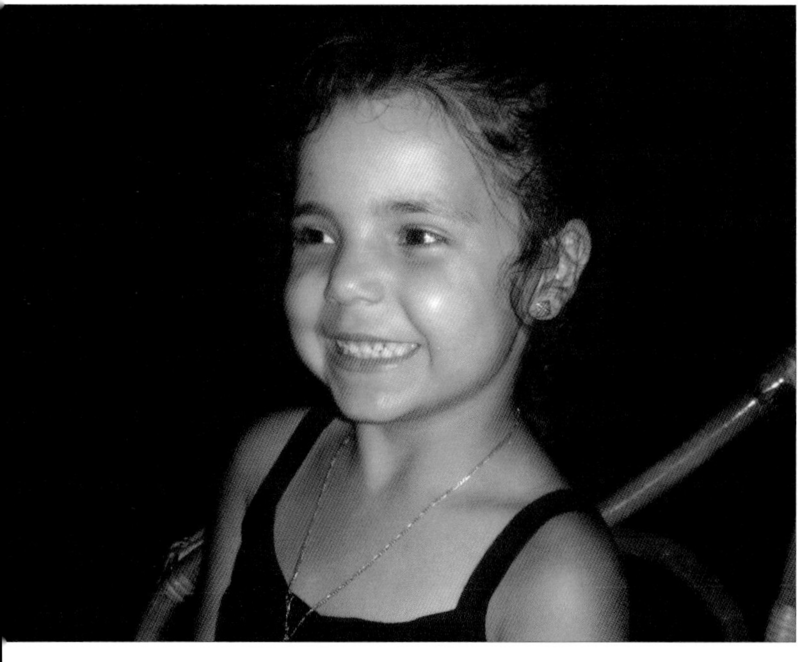

On 27 July 2007, two months to the day after Nadia was taken, I board an aeroplane heading for Tripoli, the capital of Libya. It was here I was able to spend time with Nadia, but Fawzi was always close by, even wh we were swimming in the pool.

vas important for me to keep a bit of normality in my life, but sometimes ng in such a different culture was difficult.

ove left: Lots of the streets in Libya looked the same and were in or condition.

ove right: Outside Anne Otman's house. Anne offered me a place to y out of the kindness of her heart. We often had BBQs on the rooftop her house.

low: The Watasimo organisation, run by Ayesha Gaddafi.

Libya was like a completely new world and I had to start life over again.

Above left: This was the school where I worked and the school Nadia attended before Fawzi decided to hide her. Working in the school made me feel closer to Nadia.

Above right: This was Mohammed's office, my first lawyer. You can see his filing system from floor to ceiling!

Below: This was the main courtroom – it often felt like I was living in the courtroom and most of my visits were deeply frustrating.

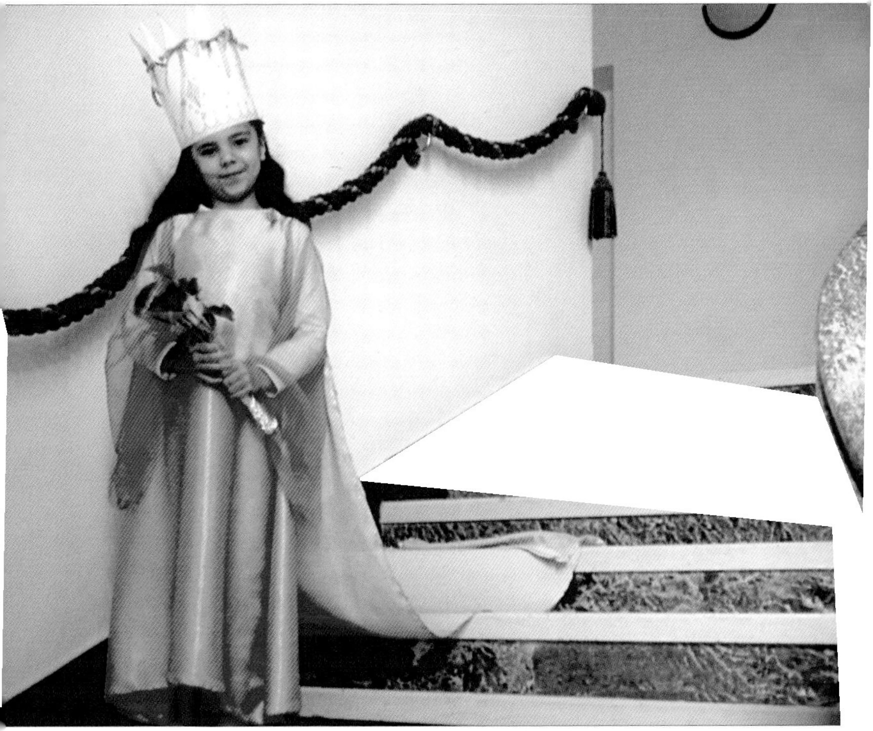

ɔove: The thought of never seeing Nadia back in the UK motivated me keep fighting for her.

·low: At the Embassy with some of the other mothers who have had ɜir children taken away from them. From left: Mufta, a voluntary ɔrker; Vincent Fean; Andrea; Tracey; Anita, who has five children living Libya; me; my mum and Theresa.

Above: From left: Arvinder, me and Andy Burnham: my two rocks.

Below: At the Embassy with (from left) Dad, Anne Fean, Mum and Arvinder.

y wonderful parents, David and Dorothy Taylor, have supported me oughout and never doubted me. Losing Nadia affected them as much it affected me, but they gave me confidence along the way and couraged me to keep going, and never give up.

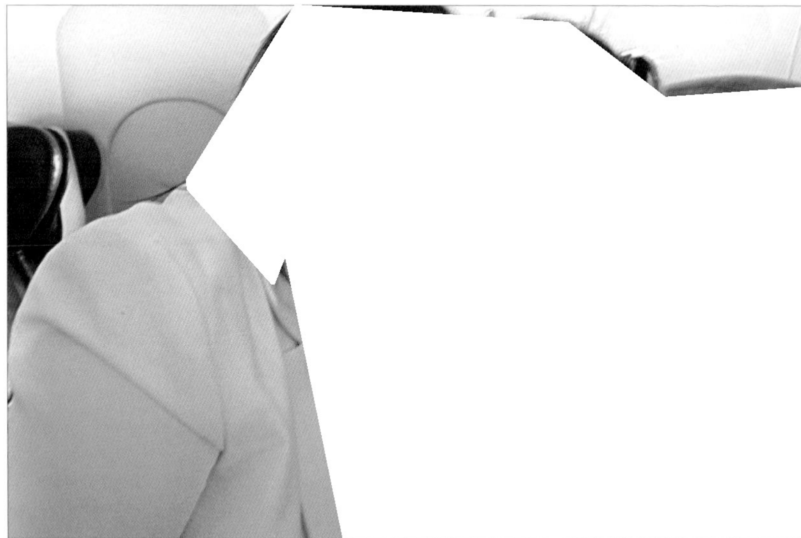

When I was finally able to take Nadia back to the UK, it was such a surreal feeling.

Above: Leaving the Embassy.

Below: On the plane home.

perhaps an attempt to discover my intentions and what I might do next?

I may have become a little paranoid, but I suppose that wasn't really surprising in the circumstances. What were these people trying to do to me, playing with my emotions? It didn't make me feel any better. Fiona did, however, provide a telephone number and said I could contact her any time for a chat. Although very dubious, I did telephone her, but I was careful what I said. I thanked Fiona for the information and told her I would be extremely grateful if she could discover anything else. I didn't mention that I was thinking about coming over to live in Libya and applying for custody, just in case Fawzi was behind this communication. Fiona advised that it would be very difficult for me in Libya as it was a patriarchal society, very much 'a man's world over here', and she doubted I would get Nadia back on my own. She didn't know what my plan was, and I certainly wasn't about to tell her.

A friend of Fiona's contacted me by email a few days later; her name was Sally Awzi. Immediately I became suspicious – even her surname was similar to Fawzi's name! Again, I was very wary of what I wrote in my emails to her. Sally also reported that she saw Nadia every day because her son was coincidentally in the same nursery-school class. She reported that Nadia was dressed smartly and was being well looked after.

This time I was happier to hear from someone who had actually seen Nadia, and it was obviously good to hear that she was well. It was also very useful information in tracking Nadia down if that's what I had to do, but part of me felt angry: it was my job to look after my daughter, not some distant relative in Tripoli.

I tried to put it all together in my mind. Fawzi took Nadia to Libya but now his sister and mother were looking after her. He was obviously 'playing the father role' when he had to, just as he had when we were together. I knew that Fawzi's sister, Mufeda, wasn't married and didn't have any children of her own. She was nearing her late thirties, and in Libya once a woman gets to this age it's hard to find a husband; because she didn't have any children of her own, she was given Nadia to look after.

A few days passed before I telephoned Fawzi again. First, I called his friend Brian in Libya and asked him to speak to Fawzi. I told him what I was planning to do and said that, if I did go to Libya, I would not be holding anything back; I had proof of him and Fawzi drinking in the UK, and all this would be discussed in any court proceedings. I had no idea whether this would influence Brian but I thought it was worth a try. Brian told me that he had had a fight with Fawzi and they were no longer speaking, but that he would speak to Fawzi's older brother, Fward.

After trawling the internet, I discovered that, once a child of a Libyan father enters the country, he or she becomes a Libyan national. I also found out that, as the mother of a Libyan child, the father has to provide for me and make available a suitable home. More importantly, under Sharia law, the moral code and religious law of Islam, the child usually resides with the mother. If I went to live in Libya and applied for custody of Nadia, it was likely that I would be successful. It would mean that I would have to leave England, set up home in Tripoli and apply to the Sharia court. So be it – that's what I would have to do. Suddenly, I sensed a solution, albeit a pretty drastic one. I was on a winning streak, and the more I researched and read up on my situation, the more I learned that the law would be on my side. I would waste no time in informing Fawzi of my plans.

A few days later, I spoke to Brian again. He didn't tell me much more other than that he had spoken to Fawzi's brother, Fward, who admitted that Fawzi had done wrong. It was clear that he and the rest of the family wouldn't go behind Fawzi's back to help me, though.

I called Fawzi again. He knew of my plan because Fward had already told him and he was very uncommunicative; he didn't think that I would have gone to such lengths. He probably thought that I would have given up by now – that's how stupid he was. The conversation then became more heated, but I grew more confident: I told him about my rights if I came to Libya, and he was clearly taken aback. I started telling him that he would need to provide for me when I arrived in Tripoli; I also told him that I had given him more than enough time to bring Nadia back home and I wasn't prepared to wait any longer. He put the phone down on me but, instead of getting cross, I now felt vindicated. It was a bit of a result. Obviously, I had hit a raw nerve and he was on the defensive.

The following day, I spoke to Nadia. Fawzi answered and put her on the phone. I told her that she would see me soon and I couldn't wait to hold her in my arms. Before she could answer, Fawzi grabbed the phone from her and fired lots of questions at me: 'How will you get your visa?' 'Where will you stay?' 'When are you coming?' He also told me that I wouldn't get into the country, and finally threatened me with: 'You will never see Nadia again!'

When Fawzi said this to me, it surprisingly didn't frighten me, it just strengthened my resolve. I calmly told him, 'Fawzi, don't fuck with me because you're fucking with the wrong person!' before hanging up. Usually, I don't swear like that and Fawzi knew it, but saying it the way I did shocked him. In a call a few days later, he was calm when I told him that I had a few things to sort out and then I'd be on my way. I didn't tell him exactly when, only that I would see him in court.

Fawzi wasn't in charge any more – I was. I felt good, positive.

My sister Steph had been a brilliant support but she was getting more and more upset at the lack of contact with Nadia and Fawzi's stubbornness. I think she had mixed emotions when I told her that I was going to Libya. She would miss me, but she admired my strength and determination; she also knew that, if I hadn't taken this decision, I would never get Nadia, her niece, back where she belonged. Steph promised me that everything would be okay and, if I needed anything, I should just ring and she would do whatever she could to help.

I sold my Suzuki Grand Vitara, which was very sad. It was only six months old and Nadia and I had loved going for trips in it. We would drive for hours, shades on, posing like Thelma and Louise! But it was all irrelevant now; it didn't mean a thing. I had bought the car brand new and so, when I went back to the garage to ask them to buy it back from me, the manager was taken aback. He couldn't understand why I wanted to sell it so quickly. I told him what had happened and he was shocked. He then asked when I was planning on going to Libya. I told him I wasn't sure yet as I had lots to do before I left. In any case, he was very considerate and we agreed a price. He was going to give me £7,000 for the car, which I was delighted with. He also told me that, when I returned the vehicle, he would lend me a courtesy car up until the day I left for Libya. I thought this was a lovely gesture and, on the way home, I had a little cry in the car.

Nadia's nursery arranged a sponsored walk to raise funds for me to go to Libya. A number of us, including some of Nadia's nursery friends, Nadia's key workers, Kara and Jessica ('Jessica Wabbit', as Nadia used to call her), completed the three-kilometre walk around the Hindley area, popping into pubs and shops and places that knew us. Dad's work also raised some money and Mum's work were very supportive and organised a fun day in aid of Nadia. It was a lovely event, with people donating prizes for the tombola and raffles. They made cakes and gave toys for a stall; they even arranged a fancy-dress football match. There were pictures of Nadia everywhere. My little princess had become a star and all this incredible support just made me even more determined to be successful in bringing her home.

My flight was leaving from Heathrow, so Donya suggested that I stay with her the night before so that we could run through any last-minute details. I also had to collect my visa from the Libyan Embassy in London. I'd had quite a lot of contact with Donya over the past few months and she had acquired the assistance of a lawyer in Tripoli. His name was Mohammed and, although he spoke only a little English, he convinced me that he was optimistic that together we could win custody of Nadia. He also said it could all be done in a month. Mohammed was extremely confident and it seemed very good news. The plan had changed and I was now going to stay in a hotel when I first arrived in Tripoli. Donya still maintained that she would join me at a later date and help me snatch Nadia back if our legal actions were unsuccessful.

Mum helped me pack my suitcase, and we were in tears the whole time. I just kept looking round the house and walking into Nadia's bedroom, cuddling her clothes, breathing in her smell. 'Mummy is coming soon, sweetheart. I'll be with you soon,' I kept saying to myself. I packed lots of things for her, including her favourite doll: Josie Jump, from the CBeebies television show

Balamory. She loved the doll and I'd even bought her a life-size yellow tracksuit exactly like Josie's.

The day finally arrived when Mum and Dad took me to the train station. I'd bought Mum two greeting cards and wrote on one:

> Everything's going to be okay, things are going to get better soon and, because you are the special person you are, I don't think it's going to take very long. I want to give you every bit of encouragement I possibly can. Believe in yourself because you really are wonderful, and don't forget beyond the clouds that sometimes get in your way, the sun is shining just for you and everything is going to be okay.

On the other I scribbled:

> So many of my thoughts are of you. Each night when the world is quiet and still, your smile and the wonderful moments we have shared crowd my mind. Each day, as I go about my routine, you slip gently into my thoughts and make me smile. Though we can't be together right now, we are together in our thoughts and memories.

I left these two little cards in an envelope in the back of Dad's car, so they would find them on the back seat after we'd parted. It was too painful to hand them over face-to-face. I tried to keep it in my head that I was only going away for a month and, before long, I would be back with their special little grandchild. On the envelope I'd written, 'Please be positive for me. I will be thinking of you all, all the time. I promise I'll be home soon with Nadia.'

Naturally, Mum kept the cards, and each time I read them a tear comes to my eye because every word is so true. I know everyone thinks they have the best parents in the world, but I can honestly say mine are. They have supported me throughout and I can't thank them enough. Without their unconditional love and support, I would never have been so strong.

I boarded the train and found my seat before placing my suitcase on the rack above my head. Looking out the window, I waved to Mum and Dad. I could see they were crying and it set me off, too. We were now all in tears. But I had no choice – I had to get Nadia back for all of us.

CHAPTER 6

The Quest Begins

'If the sun starts to move West, find a shady tree.'

Libyan Proverb

I searched through my bag again. It must be somewhere, surely? This couldn't be happening, not now, not after all I'd gone through. Where was it? I felt like I couldn't take any more disasters, but it was true: all my money had gone. By selling my car and taking out my remaining savings, I'd managed to amass £4,800 for the trip (I had to pay some bills and Donya from the money I'd made from selling the car) – but now all the cash had vanished.

On the morning of 16 November 2007, Donya had taken me to Heathrow Airport. I had a lot of luggage: a suitcase, a bag full of toys and sweets for Nadia, and my handbag containing money and important documents. I had intended using a shoulder bag to keep the money in, but Donya persuaded me to use one of her handbags. I didn't think at the time why she had done this – the shoulder bag was actually more secure – but I went along with her suggestion. I checked in and went through passport control, but was told at security that I couldn't take two pieces of hand luggage on board the plane.

The official refused to let me go through, so I took everything out of my handbag and put all the contents into my holdall. I looked for the money, which I had placed in a large white envelope, but there was no sign of it. Had I put the envelope on a table earlier? I didn't know. My head was all over the place. Apart from a tiny amount of English money, every single penny had disappeared. All the money that I needed to support myself and Nadia had been lifted. Cold with fright, I double-checked my bag, but it still wasn't there.

I rang Donya as soon as I realised I had lost all my cash. She was really upset for me and offered to return to Heathrow. The airport authorities let me meet her, although I had gone through passport control, and Donya gave me £140 that she had just withdrawn from a cash machine. She told me to board the plane and she would send more money over once I was in Tripoli; she never did.

This was unbelievable: things couldn't get any worse. All I could think was: *I'm not a bad person, what can I possibly have done wrong to be punished like this?* There was nothing I could do at this stage – I just had to carry on. I boarded the plane and cried all the way to Tripoli.

Mohammed, the lawyer whom Donya had engaged, met me at the airport with his friend, Ali. Mohammed's English wasn't the best, but we could communicate. If I had to describe Mohammed, I would say he reminded me of the Nutty Professor! He was very large and would sweat profusely. I liked him straight away – he seemed like a genuine person and I felt he really wanted to help me.

The two men took me to a hotel, where I could exchange the small amount of British Sterling that I had luckily kept in my purse into Libyan dinar. They then drove me to the hotel, where I would be staying. It seemed okay. Not exactly five-star luxury, but it would do the job. It was in a nondescript area, although it was near to the sea and I later discovered that it wasn't far from the British Embassy, which was reassuring.

I walked into the entrance and checked in, having handed over my passport to two men sitting behind the counter. The heat was incredible and Mohammed stayed in the car. Ali, who didn't speak any English, took my luggage out of the van and brought it into reception. There was a large seating area and lots of men smoking; I didn't see any women at all and I felt a little intimidated as they were looking at me. I had decided not to wear a headscarf because that just wasn't me, but I hoped they didn't feel offended.

My room was on the second floor and Ali and I squeezed ourselves and my luggage into a tiny lift. He was already making me feel uncomfortable as he was constantly looking at me and smiling. I gave him the benefit of the doubt, hoped that he was just being nice and smiled back. He brought the bags into my room and indicated that he would be back at 7pm with some food, which I thought was very nice of him, especially as I didn't want to leave the hotel that evening.

I viewed my accommodation. It was a small and very basic room, with an uncomfortable-looking bed. The television was falling to pieces and the curtains looked as if they hadn't been washed for years. There was no carpet, only a small rug. The door to my room wasn't quite flush to the wall, and I had trouble closing it properly. I felt a little insecure, so I bolted the door and made sure it was locked at all times. From then on, every night I wedged my case against the door for extra security. One good thing was that there was an ensuite bathroom and shower.

At 7pm, Ali returned with pizza and chips, and a Libyan sim card for my mobile phone. I thanked him and showed him the door, but, instead of leaving, he stroked my hair and asked if he could kiss me. I shoved him away and told him to leave me alone. He said, 'Mohammed, no kiss!' I think he was trying to tell me that I shouldn't tell Mohammed that he had tried to kiss me. He left, looking worried. I sat down on the bed, feeling sick. What kind of place was this? I'd only been there a couple of hours and a man had already violated me and assumed as a Western woman I was easy meat. *The sooner I get Nadia and get out of here, the better*, I thought.

Mohammed had told me earlier that I should have Nadia in a week. I sincerely hoped so. I rang home and informed Mum and Dad that I had been robbed. They already knew – Donya had rung my mum at work to tell her. Mum burst into tears and couldn't see how I could possibly manage in Libya with so little money. I knew that they were tempted to tell me to come home and rethink my plans, but they also knew that they couldn't do that; no matter what, they knew that I wouldn't listen to them. My parents promised to send me £200 immediately. From then on, they sent me money each month for the rest of my stay. Bless them!

The following morning, I got up, feeling totally gutted. I still couldn't believe someone could take my money like that. I had no idea how I was going to manage. Mohammed did say his sister knew of a job in a school, though.

I needed to tell everyone at home that I had arrived safely, so I took a cab to the town centre and found an internet café, where I emailed all the family. I couldn't wait to get started on my quest to find Nadia and took another cab to Souk al Juma, the suburb where Fawzi lived, to see if I could find the house where we went in July. When I visited the family home on my first visit to Libya, I had filmed the route on my video camera, just in case I couldn't remember it. Since that trip, I had watched it a number of times so I had some idea of where to go; I also remembered that the building was near the monument on the five-dinar bank note. I instructed the taxi driver as best as I could to locate the monument and he left me there. At a main junction, I turned and crossed a busy dual carriageway.

I trekked all the way down a main road for about a mile to see if anything else looked familiar. It was called Arada Road and everyone was staring at me; men in their cars were beeping their horns at me. But I didn't care – I just needed to find the house where Nadia was staying. The neighbourhood was quite poor and rundown; it didn't feel particularly safe. After further exploration, I came upon what I thought was the right street. There was no road; instead, the house was on a dirt track, the last in a row of about eight other houses, all on one side of the road. Opposite were palm trees and there were no streetlights, so at night it was very dark.

I had been advised that buildings in Tripoli didn't possess proper addresses, so if you want to find someone you have to ask a neighbour. Everything was done by word of mouth, but I studied what I thought was Fawzi's house. I looked around for clothes on the washing line that might belong to Nadia but I couldn't see anything. A three-storey property, the entrance was fronted by tall metal gates; I wasn't absolutely 100 per cent sure that this was the right property, though, and I didn't want to be knocking at the wrong door and create trouble with neighbours. I was also feeling very nervous – I had only just arrived in the country and there was the chance that Fawzi might have me arrested, or maybe even keep me prisoner in the house. At this point, I decided to return to the city centre.

Later, I discovered that I was absolutely right: it had been Fawzi's house. I had found it but with hindsight it's probably just as well that I didn't burst in on the family. Who knows what might have happened?

I had arranged a meeting with Mohammed that afternoon. At first, I wasn't impressed with the set-up. His cramped office had very little furniture or equipment – just a few chairs and a small wooden table. I remember thinking my office back home was luxurious compared to this. Another room had filing cabinets from floor to ceiling, crammed with orange files, which were also all over the floor. It was clear that the system needed some attention. Still, the mess did make me think he was a genuine lawyer.

I gave Mohammed the documents he required. He seemed more than happy with all the information I had provided and was amazed at what Fawzi had been up to while in the UK. I informed Mohammed that I thought I had found Fawzi's house, which he was pleased about because court orders could be served on him at the address. What I didn't tell Mohammed was that I had lost my money. I just explained that I had very little cash on me at the time and wouldn't be able to pay him any more at that stage. Mohammed stated this wasn't a problem as we had already given some money upfront, arranged by

Donya. He advised me not to try to see Nadia in case it affected the court hearings. I didn't tell him how close I had been to doing just that earlier that morning! Mohammed added that he would apply to the court for access visits initially and, following this, we would press for full custody. He seemed quite positive about my custody application, although he obviously couldn't tell me how long it might take. The trouble was he didn't know how difficult a character Fawzi was. He also warned that, even if I was awarded custody of Nadia, I would have to remain in the country. At that stage, I didn't care – we would find a way around that, if necessary – I just wanted my daughter back.

While I was there, I also met Mohammed's sister, who was actually in charge of the law firm. Some of the more liberal Libyan families allow their womenfolk to work, and she was in the fortunate position of being given such freedom. She assured me that, with their help, we would eventually win the custody battle. I hated to think that Nadia was the subject of a battle, but this is what Fawzi had initiated and, if he wanted a fight, I would scrap with him to the bitter end. Feeling much more optimistic, I returned to the hotel. Already I had achieved quite a lot in twenty-four hours, I felt.

Despite my promising start, that first week was difficult. There were no shops or supermarkets nearby and I was very conscious about spending what little money I had, so I decided to limit myself to one meal a day. I mainly stayed in my room – I wondered if any of the neighbours had told Fawzi I was in Libya and began to think that he might be looking for me. Probably paranoid, but then who wouldn't be in my position? My initial hopeful mood turned to pessimism as I began to spend too much time on my own; obsessing in my mind over what had brought me to this place.

Although we spoke on the phone most days for the first month or so, Donya never visited me in Libya as she had promised. This, she explained, was because her passport had been cancelled and she was unable to leave the country. She also said that, if the Libyan authorities got wind of my plan, she would be arrested. I never knew how true this was – perhaps it was her excuse for extricating herself from any further involvement and she had no intention of coming to see me at all.

One day, I decided to contact the British Embassy. One of the staff, Linda, told me that I was welcome to come in for a chat any time if ever I felt lonely or isolated. Although grateful for her offer, I thought I needed more than just 'a chat' – I felt quite low. I was so close to Nadia, yet so far away. In any case, I made an appointment to see the Vice Consul of the British Embassy.

This was when I first met Arvinder Vohra, who turned out to be an incredibly important person over the next few years. At first I thought he was Libyan – dark-skinned, tall and attractive – but he was British of Indian parentage. He told me that, although sympathetic, the Consulate couldn't become embroiled in the legal situation with Nadia, but they could look out for my safety and help in any other way. I broke down in tears and begged him for help; he was incredibly understanding but I needed more. I went to a café and treated myself to chicken and rice – a little comfort eating – but it was no good; I just ran out into a nearby backstreet, sat on the pavement and sobbed and sobbed.

This was only my first week and already I was struggling. I telephoned Fiona, the only other person in Libya who I knew, and who had emailed me when I was in England. I needed someone who I could talk to in Libya – I don't think I had ever felt so lonely. Fiona's response was brilliant. She was incredibly upbeat and promised to meet me that same evening.

Fiona collected me from the hotel and took me back to her house for dinner. She was lovely and very welcoming, and, because I was a bit nervous about meeting her, immediately put me at my ease. I needed someone to talk to in my own language and she couldn't have been nicer. Despite this, I was careful about what I said because I still found it hard to trust anyone completely. I met her Libyan husband, who was very sympathetic. Neither of them could believe what Fawzi had done nor that he was apparently getting away with it; I told them I was there to make sure he didn't get away with it. While I was at their house, Fiona rang her friend Sally, whose son attended the same nursery school as Nadia, and we arranged to spend the following day together.

As Fiona had done the previous day, Sally collected me and took me back to her house. I got on really well with her and she told me about that first encounter with Nadia. Several weeks ago, Sally had been at an indoor playground, which Nadia had told me about, with her son, Hussain, and had heard a little girl speaking English to her father in a broad Lancashire accent! Intrigued, she became even more so when there was no sign of the little girl's mother. She asked the father where his wife was and he replied that she was in London, looking after her sick father; she would shortly be joining them in Libya. Sally became suspicious and actually confronted Fawzi, accusing him of kidnapping the little girl. This was pretty brave of her – to tackle a complete stranger and accuse him of such a crime – but thank goodness she did! Of course, Fawzi denied it but, surprisingly, before he left the playground, he actually admitted to Sally that he had kidnapped Nadia and even handed her one of his business cards. Always on the prowl – no matter what the circumstance!

That night, Sally went home and did some research. Online, she discovered all about Nadia. After that, she and Fiona decided to email me, having discovered that her son Hussain and Nadia were in the same class at nursery school. Sally had seen her at school and said Nadia was obviously being well cared for, but seemed more withdrawn. I was pleased to hear that my daughter was in good health and being looked after properly, but a little concerned that she had lost her sparkle.

At least I now knew where Nadia was living and where she attended school. I was getting closer, but there was nothing I could do to get her back. My thoughts had turned to snatching her, but Mohammed had warned that, if I did anything silly, I could end up in jail and worse – back in Britain without Nadia.

Being with Sally that day really helped me to feel a bit more positive. Her Englishness made me feel less of a stranger in a foreign land – she was really lovely. I met her husband Abi and her three children; they were a great family. It was to be just the start of our relationship.

The following morning, Sally made me an offer I couldn't refuse; she rang and told me to get my luggage together. She wanted me to come and stay with her and her family for as long as I needed until I had sorted myself out. I was incredibly grateful, but I'm a very independent person and I don't like to rely on other people, especially those I don't even know – I've always been like it. But it was a wonderful gesture and I couldn't believe how kind she and her family were being, so I accepted graciously and moved out of the hotel, relieved.

Fiona and her husband took me back for another meeting with Mohammed. He had made an application to the court for access visits and was awaiting judgment. I had received some money from home and gave him a further 500 dinars (about £250) for his services. After that, I was almost in daily contact and never gave the poor man a moment's respite from my demands.

A few weeks later, Mohammed's hard work and my constant haranguing paid off when he rang to say I had been granted permission to see Nadia every Saturday at

Fawzi's house – but just for two hours. My first reaction was one of relief that something was happening, but this quickly turned to anger. I knew Mohammed was doing his best, but I was livid when I thought about the ruling more clearly. *Two hours a week was nothing! I was being unduly punished for something I hadn't done.* To add insult to injury, the first visit was planned for 8 December, nearly two weeks away.

The wait was unbearable. Sally, Fiona and their families were incredibly supportive. Sally introduced me to her friend Anne Otman, who worked as a secretary at the British Embassy. Anne couldn't believe that the Embassy hadn't provided an official to accompany me and was worried that I might be at risk if I went on the access visit unaccompanied so she very thoughtfully agreed to take me to Fawzi's house to make it look more official. Anne had a British Consulate ID badge, so having her involvement would make Fawzi think that the visit was an official diplomatic arrangement.

When the day finally arrived, I was incredibly nervous. The visit had been arranged between 4pm and 6pm, and Sally took me to Anne's house, as planned. I'd brought loads of presents and games from home that I hoped Nadia would remember. I wasn't allowed to take her away from Fawzi's family's house and I knew that I was going to be watched like a hawk while I was there, which was bound to make me feel uncomfortable, but I didn't care so long as I was able to see to see my daughter. I would have done anything. It was also strange that no one had informed me officially of the address – it was only by my earlier detective work that I knew how to direct Anne.

We arrived at the house at exactly 4pm. Fawzi answered the door and was surprised to see Anne. He immediately asked who she was and Anne piped up confidently, 'I'm from the British Embassy and I have brought Sarah to see Nadia. I will be collecting Sarah at 6pm.' This scheme worked really well – Fawzi didn't have a clue it was an informal arrangement and that Anne was only there out of the kindness of her heart.

Reluctantly, he showed me into the house. Then I heard a voice shout out, 'Mummy, *Mummy*!' As I looked up the stairs, I saw Nadia excitedly calling out my name. After all these months, I was overwhelmed to see my little girl. I had endured recurring fantasies that she wouldn't recognise me so her words were wonderful to hear. Taking my arm, she showed me upstairs and asked me to remove my shoes, which I did. She showed me into a lounge-type room full of mendars (large foam cushions), which were placed around the room to sit on instead of chairs. They were covered with brightly coloured material. Later, I was told that the quality of these mendars denoted how rich the family was – these were not at all luxurious.

Nadia was in pyjamas and had her hair in a ponytail; I always used to wonder who did her hair when I wasn't around. I sat talking with my daughter until all her cousins came into the room and glared at me. I'd bought Nadia some sweets and let her choose her favourite ones.

I was now being watched by Fawzi's brother, mother and sister – all making sure I didn't put a foot out of line. It was obvious I wasn't going to have any quality time alone with Nadia because of everyone being around, but for now I didn't care so long as I was with her.

I was given a drink of juice, but I didn't touch it at first as I wasn't sure whether one of them might have spiked it. However, there were two glasses of juice and I doubted they would poison Nadia – they didn't know which glass she would take. I figured it was probably safe and so I took a gulp. Then Fawzi came into the room and started asking me questions: where was I living and when was I going home? He also enquired when my visa ran out. I told him it was none of his business; I was in Libya for as long as I wanted, and I was there to see Nadia so he should leave me alone because I only had two hours a week with her. I didn't want to argue in front of Nadia, and, when Fawzi realised that he wasn't going to get anything out of me, he backed off and went to sit in another room from where he could still see me. I didn't let him see that I was nervous and just carried on playing with Nadia.

When the two hours was up, I told Nadia I loved her very much and that I would be back the following week, adding, 'You will always be in Mummy's heart.' I pointed to her heart and she responded by saying, 'I love you too, Mummy.' Then I waved goodbye and she came back twice to give me a hug, as if she didn't want to let me go. Putting on a brave face, I told her to be a good girl and said I would see her very soon. She went inside, and Fawzi and his brother, Fward, escorted me from the house. They tried to make me feel threatened and acted as if they were some kind of gangsters but I just held my head high and walked out.

Anne was outside waiting for me but, just as I was about to get in the car, Fawzi came running out. 'What have you given Nadia? Have you poisoned her?' he screamed.

I ran back into the house to see Nadia crying and bending over the toilet, while Fawzi's mother and sister, Mufeda, looked on. I asked what the problem was and Fawzi accused me of poisoning my own daughter. Nadia ran straight into my arms, crying. I told Fawzi that it was his fault, he was upsetting her – 'That's why she's sick, she doesn't want me to go!'

Fawzi told Nadia to be quiet. At that moment I hated him more than I thought possible.

As I climbed into the car in tears, barely able to keep my temper, Anne told me she had spoken to Fawzi's brother, who told her that he was keen to sort this mess out. I hoped so, and thought at least one of the family members had shown some sense.

Sally, Anne and I had arranged that, when Anne came to collect me, we wouldn't go straight back to Sally's but would make a detour so that, if we were followed, Fawzi wouldn't know where I was staying. Anne took me to another girl's house in the suburbs. Mary lived in a block of flats so that, if someone saw me enter the building, they wouldn't know which flat I was going into. Mary was really nice and had a young daughter of her own. She couldn't believe what I was going through and, like everyone I'd met so far, was very supportive.

Anne left and Sally collected me. Mary and Sally dressed me in a hijab and scarf, just showing my eyes, so that I could walk from the block of flats to Sally's car (Sally had a daughter of eighteen, so I could easily pass for her). We drove back to Sally's house, feeling safe, and we decided to continue with this plan when I visited Nadia every Saturday.

I wasn't allowed to see Nadia outside the hours agreed by the court, but, during the week while I was waiting for my next visit, Sally introduced me to Nadia's teacher. Her name was Patricia – she was a lovely woman from Scotland, but had married a Libyan and converted to Islam, so she wears a headscarf. Patricia told me Nadia was fine and doing okay at school, although she added that the class had been having a discussion about Christmas the other day and Nadia got a little upset as she told her classmates that she had had to leave all her toys in England. Having raised the topic, Patricia had felt a little guilty about this but in the end Nadia was fine about it. She was astonished when I told her what had happened to Nadia.

I asked Patricia if she would do me a great favour and tell Nadia that Mummy is in her heart and point to her heart – I wanted Nadia to know that, although I might not always be with her physically, I was always thinking of her. This was a gesture that we both used regularly and something that I would always say to Nadia. Patricia agreed to do it for me. I didn't tell Patricia, but, now that I knew where Nadia was at school, I began to think that I could sneak into the building and snatch her. *I could get a taxi and head for the Tunisian border*. The more I thought about it, the more I felt sick with fear. *Could it work? But what would happen if it all went wrong?*

The following Saturday, I went to see Nadia again. This time Anne's daughter, Hanna, dropped me off. Nadia greeted me, although she seemed a little subdued. Perhaps she had been ordered not to get too close to me? She wasn't as affectionate as she had been the week before, and I didn't get any kisses or cuddles. After about half an hour, Fawzi appeared and started firing questions at me again. I tried to ignore him. He then persuaded Nadia to tell me she now lived with Daddy and liked Libya. It was obvious that a four-year-old wouldn't say this without coercion. This just reinforced my belief that Fawzi was doing all he could to get back at me and that he wasn't at all bothered about Nadia's needs.

During the visit, I took some pictures of Nadia, which he wasn't happy about, but he didn't try to stop me. I then asked his permission for Nadia to talk to my mum and dad in England but he refused point blank. I asked why, but, before he could answer, his mum and sister (who had joined us) spoke to him in Arabic. After a heated conversation, they must have convinced him there was no harm in Nadia being allowed to talk to her grandparents, so he agreed to this request – so long as the conversation could be heard on loudspeaker. Luckily, Nana and Granddad were at home and they had a short conversation with their granddaughter. I could tell they were thrilled to hear Nadia again and I was really delighted that she recognised their voices.

The two hours went incredibly quickly and it was time to say our farewells. I left, promising Nadia that I would see her again. This time around, she was less upset – there were no tears and, although I was pleased she wasn't unhappy, I did wonder if Fawzi had forbidden her to cry.

That week, I thought more about secretly whisking Nadia from school to try to take her out of Libya. I couldn't stand to see the way her father was treating her and how he was using her to get back at me; I knew she would be happier with my family and me in England. Aware that Nadia was attending school regularly, all I needed to do was choose a date to make my move. I decided that a Thursday would be best as it was the last working day of the week – it seemed that nothing much happens on that day because everyone is winding down and I thought, if everyone was slightly more relaxed, I might make it across the border to Tunisia a little more easily. I decided that Thursday, 29 December 2007 would be the day I'd attempt to carry out my plan. All week I was very nervous and I still couldn't think straight. I confided in Sally, who was horrified and absolutely certain that this was the wrong thing to do; she kept telling me not to try anything so stupid. At the time, I felt it had been easy for her to take that view: she wasn't in my position. I was miserable and I wanted to get out of Libya with Nadia, but I was equally sick with fear that, if I failed, I could end up in prison and might never see my daughter again. For those few days, my head was spinning with all the possible outcomes.

When the day arrived, I hadn't slept a wink. I wasn't thinking straight, I couldn't eat; I was shaking with fear. Sally and her husband, Abi, were still giving me a hard time for considering such a plan and repeated that, if it all went wrong, I would be jailed, kicked out of the country and never be able to return. I just didn't know what to do, or which way to turn; I wasn't functioning properly. I couldn't breathe, I was in complete meltdown – it was like I was being suffocated. I just wanted to get out of there. In the end, I couldn't do it. The day of the intended snatching passed in a blur.

I was still feeling disorientated the next day, 22 December 2007, the date of my next visit to Nadia. Another friend, Sue, who I had made through Sally, took me to Fawzi's house. I had scarcely entered the home, or greeted Nadia, when Fawzi started interrogating me: 'How long are you staying? Where are you living? When does your visa run out? Why are you doing this to my family?'

I told him that I wasn't there to answer his questions – I had only two hours with Nadia and I wanted to see her properly. He dragged Nadia away into another room and I followed. Fawzi told me that he wasn't going to let me be with Nadia that day. Angrily, he told his sister,

Mufeda, to take Nadia away and get her dressed. Mufeda started shouting at him. I begged Fawzi to let me just spend five minutes with my daughter. At this point, Fawzi grabbed me by the throat and forced me up against a wall – I don't know what he would have done to me, but luckily Mufeda started screaming and dragged him off me. He grabbed Nadia again and took her away. I wanted to follow them, but I was afraid of what might happen and I didn't want Nadia to witness such a scene. I rang Mohammed, who told me to go to the police station and report the incident. Then I rang Sue and waited for her to collect me. Shaken, I told her what had happened. We drove to a police station, but, after waiting for a while, we were told that we were at the wrong place and given directions for another police station nearby.

When we arrived, I was shocked to see Fawzi and his brother Fward already in conversation with an officer. Fawzi told him that I had attempted to snatch Nadia and his story was corroborated by Fward, who hadn't even been there! Sue spoke some Arabic and we tried to explain that Fawzi had actually attacked me, but it seemed they were taking his side. Sue rang her daughter, Camilla, who knew someone in the police and intervened on our behalf. We were advised that, if we stuck to our stories, both Fawzi and I would be sent to jail, pending police enquiries. I realised that this wasn't going to help anyone and so we dropped the accusation, as did Fawzi.

The following day, a meeting was arranged to try to sort out the situation. A representative of Watasimo,

Ayesha Gaddafi's charity, was there as a neutral observer, and on my side were Mohammed and Farouk, a British Embassy official who also acted as an interpreter. Fawzi was accompanied by his lawyer, and several friends and family members – a large entourage, all there clearly to try to intimidate me. Although Farouk did his best, it was difficult to follow the proceedings because the conversation was flowing thick and fast. Basically, Fawzi admitted to what he'd done, but said it would never happen again and I was welcome back to see Nadia every Saturday at his house, as agreed by the court. In return, I told them that I was too frightened to return there as I couldn't trust Fawzi and feared for my safety. I demanded to see Nadia on neutral ground, where we could spend time together without the threat of violence. Mohammed was to negotiate this with Fawzi's lawyer informally, but, in the meantime, continue with the custody application.

Mohammed rang me later that week to say that he hadn't been able to arrange an informal meeting for the following Saturday and we would have to go back to court to sort out future access meetings. I was devastated. I'd only had two proper visits with Nadia and the third had been a disaster. We were back to square one. Christmas was a pretty miserable affair and, despite Sally and her family's best attempts to cheer me up, I wondered where, and when, all this was going to end. Despite my daily phone calls to Mohammed, and constant contact with the Embassy, there were no further court hearings in January. It felt like I was going backwards, having achieved so much in the first few weeks after my arrival in Libya.

Then suddenly, out of the blue, I had some amazing news. In February 2008, Mohammed rang me at Sally's. There had been no court appearance but we had won the case, and I had been awarded custody of Nadia! At last, I was to be reunited with my daughter. Mohammed then dropped a bombshell: this was not a final decision and Fawzi had a right to appeal. Nadia would not be placed with me in the meantime; she would remain with Fawzi and his family. Worse still, Fawzi was opposing the access arrangements, so I was to be denied access to Nadia for the time being.

Week after week, we went to court but nothing was happening to get me closer to seeing Nadia. My lawyer wasn't able to achieve anything, and it seemed Fawzi had the upper hand. I was now worse off than ever before and Fawzi used every trick in the book to prolong the case. He accused me of being a drunk, and of being unfit to be a mother; he even said I was dying of leukaemia – so I had to get Mum and Dad to provide evidence from my doctor to deny Fawzi's claims. But all this took up valuable time and I had no contact with Nadia; I was out of my mind with worry and missing her so much.

Looking back, I realise that nearly all my time during this period was taken up with my obsession with Nadia and working out ways to get her back. I must have driven everyone mad, and it's amazing that Sally and her family and friends put up with me for so long. In the end, I stayed with Sally for nine months. Talk about '*The Man Who Came To Dinner*'! I did my best to fit in quietly with their routine as much as possible, but I also tried to keep a low profile. I didn't want anyone finding out where I was living; in Tripoli, it seemed everyone knew everyone else's business.

There wasn't much of a social life for women in Libya, but we did what we could. Most mornings were spent food shopping or visiting Sally's friends, some of whom became my friends. On Monday evenings, Sally would invite 'the girls' over – a group of British women, all married to Libyans and living in Tripoli. Sally made a buffet of pizzas, *burek* (small mince pasties) and some cakes for dessert. Inevitably, my conversation revolved around the latest court appearances or news of Nadia. I liked to be with Sarah and Hussain, Sally's two youngest children, cooking together or playing hide and seek – I think it was these kids that kept me sane. They were so affectionate; they would tell me all the time that they loved me and they were sure Nadia loved me, too. It meant so much. At weekends, we would sometimes go to the seaside and pass the time at a private beach just for foreigners, where no Libyans were allowed and so we didn't have to cover our bodies. It was lovely and I spent a lot of time there, mainly thinking about Nadia.

If we didn't go to the beach, Anne would invite us to a clubhouse, which belonged to the British Embassy. There was a fantastic swimming pool and a seating area where we could chill. The atmosphere was so different to anywhere else that it didn't feel like I was in Libya when I was there: a proper oasis.

On Thursdays, the last working day of the week, we would go to a little supermarket outlet called Morjan for a coffee. They also sold the best hot cocoa ever and chocolate *cinnabon*, which are like doughnuts, with hot chocolate sauce oozing out of the centre. I can still taste them now! We would all meet there – the same girls from Sally's Monday nights – and put the world to rights. There was a small supermarket nearby, as well as a few other shops, including an expensive jewellery store; also a small toy emporium. Every time I went in there with Sarah and Hussain, I would always imagine taking Nadia there and buying the entire stock.

There were no pubs or clubs to go to and most of the customers in cafés were men. If a single woman went into one of those cafés, she would be stared at and hassled so it wasn't worth the trouble. As you might guess, I sometimes found it hard to keep my mouth shut and, if I was stared at or bothered by a strange man, I would always tell him to leave me alone. If that didn't work, by then I had learned some choice Arabic phrases and swear words!

I remember one day coming back in a taxi and, as I was getting out, the driver touched me up. I swore at him in Arabic but he just laughed, like it was the normal thing to do. This wasn't the first time I had been touched; the Arab men all believed that Western women were easy. On lots of occasions when I was out with Sally, men would throw their mobile phone numbers on scraps of paper into our car. It was as if they drove around the streets of Tripoli with a pile of such notes on the seat next to them, in case they saw likely looking women drive past! Another time I was out walking with a friend in town when a man in a car followed us up and down several streets. I'd had enough of it and stopped and called out to him: 'What do you want?' He turned the whole thing around and said it was *me* who wanted something. As if! I pulled my phone out of my pocket, took a picture of him and threatened to report him. He drove off, and we never saw him again. It was all very annoying. I know girls and women are harassed in England, too, but there wasn't a day that went by in Libya without a man making some kind of sexual remark. In the end, I just had to learn to ignore it. Not easy for me and my big mouth!

During this time, I also stayed with Anne Otman for a while. Every year, Sally returned home to the UK to see her family and we decided it would be best for me to stay with Anne for the time she was away. She lived quite close to Sally's and I was beginning to get to know the neighbourhood quite well. Anne made the best potato pie, which reminded me of the dish my grandma used to make, and she also had crockery that my nana used to have. It made me feel close to home – I believed Nana was watching over me while I was in Libya.

I realised that, while I was away, it was very difficult for the family I had left behind. From the occasional contact I had with them, I knew they were missing me and concerned for my safety. Through the various setbacks, Mum would get upset and my dad became frustrated and angry; their relationship was sorely tested during this time. My brother Andy was brilliant and tried to keep the others as calm as possible. He always tried to stay optimistic and find something positive to try to move forward. I knew he found it hard to keep strong for the family, especially as he was under no illusions about the pain I was going through and could see how the situation was affecting the whole family.

As I said, in the months after I had gained custody of Nadia, we went to court very regularly – sometimes weekly or fortnightly – and the case was adjourned numerous times while Fawzi played for time. Finally, in June, I was awarded a court order, which stated I had permission to fetch Nadia from Fawzi's house. It had taken a ridiculous amount of time from the date that I had been granted custody, but at last I was going to get my daughter back. Fawzi hadn't been informed of the ruling, so it was agreed that I would go to the local police station and be accompanied by officers in case he became aggressive, which was more than likely – I was in no doubt about this. Camilla also came with me to interpret.

We climbed aboard a police van with a couple of officers and drove the short distance to Fawzi's house. The police knocked on the imposing steel gates and Fawzi's mother, Mona, appeared. She opened the gates and then let the officers through the front door of the house. They asked Mona where Nadia was, and she replied that Fawzi and Nadia no longer lived at that address. I insisted that the police officers search the house – I wanted to do it myself, but they wouldn't let me inside.

When the policemen came out of the house, they told Camilla that there was no sign Nadia was still living in the house – there were no clothes, no toys, absolutely nothing of hers. Fawzi's mum also came outside and looked at me with a smile on her face. I said to her in Arabic that Allah was watching her and that one day she would be punished.

I couldn't understand why Nadia wasn't there nor how the family seemed to know we were coming that day. Apart from my friends, only the police were aware of the plan. It was obvious that Fawzi must have known we were coming and been tipped off somehow.

Fawzi was now hiding Nadia, and it seemed he was being helped in this way by an insider. I had been granted custody, but I hadn't seen my daughter for six months and I had no idea where she was. Terrible thoughts swept through my mind – my worst fear being that Fawzi might have harmed her and she had been the victim of an 'honour killing'. *Surely Fawzi couldn't even contemplate murdering his own daughter?* But then I was bringing disgrace to the family and the easiest way to stop all this would be to commit an evil act such as this. I just had to reassure myself that he wouldn't do it, but these nightmarish fantasies made me more determined to find Nadia.

CHAPTER 7

Following the Leader

I had first met Sir Vincent Fean, the British Ambassador, when Mum and I visited Libya on the International Social Services trip, and he had invited me and the other mums to the residence for the day. He had been very sympathetic but had stressed that he was unable to use diplomatic means to return Nadia to me because she was a Libyan child. Since I had been living in Tripoli on a permanent basis, I had seen Vincent or his deputy once or twice a month and had probably made weekly phone calls to Vincent or Arvinder Vohra, the Vice Consul of the British Embassy. They always made time for me and were a great source of support, as were other members of staff.

On 9 July 2008, Sally and I were invited to a garden

party at the Embassy, given by Vincent Fean's wife, Anne. She was a lovely woman – very tall and slim, down-to-earth – and I liked her immediately. Anne Fean introduced us to two women. One didn't speak a word of English, but the other, Sana, was quite chatty and spoke fluent English. Sana told me that they were personal assistants to Colonel Muammar Gaddafi, Libya's infamous President. In fact, the PA who couldn't speak English was actually Gaddafi's cousin.

I couldn't believe it! If anyone in the world could help me, it must be President Gaddafi, the Leader. What was I to do? We sat down and I told them the whole story from the beginning, including the fact that I had won custody back in February, but I still didn't have Nadia.

I had asked my mum and dad to look out for some press cuttings from the local newspaper, which reported the charges laid against Fawzi while in Wigan so I could arm myself with evidence, should it be required in Libya. Wherever I went, I carried these with me in case I needed to prove what kind of a person Fawzi was. I showed them to Sana, who was genuinely shocked. She asked if I had a copy of the custody order, which I also carried around with me. I went off to photocopy the paperwork she needed and gave it to her. She said that she would do all she could to get me a meeting with the Leader. I was dumbstruck. This was brilliant – the first piece of good luck since I'd arrived in Libya! I gave Sana my number and she said she would call me later. There was even the possibility that I could go and see the Colonel the next day. After midnight, I got a call from Sana; the meeting was definitely on for the following day. She said she would ring me to confirm everything and I should be ready to leave at any time.

Believe it or not, I actually had doubts about meeting with Colonel Gaddafi. I'd been told that, once an arrangement had been made with him, it could not be broken; there was no going back. It suddenly dawned on me: this was the most powerful man in Libya and, if he decided I didn't have the right to have Nadia and, as a Libyan citizen, she shouldn't be placed with a British woman, he might then instruct the courts accordingly. No one would disobey him. Perhaps I should just let the legal case come to fruition. But then again, I wasn't getting any nearer gaining access to Nadia, and it was all just dragging on. I realised that I must meet with Gaddafi and trust my initial instincts. At every turn during my stay in Libya, I was faced with these sorts of decisions and I was always racked with uncertainty: was I doing the right thing, and what was best for Nadia?

The following day, 10 July – my birthday – I didn't feel like celebrating, even though I'd had a bit of a breakthrough. Without Nadia, all birthdays and every Christmas were put on hold. But then, around lunchtime, I got a call from Sana to advise me that the encounter with Gaddafi had been postponed. Another disappointment, but only temporary this time as the meeting was duly arranged to take place a few days later. Arrangements had been made for about ten of us to go, including a number of other women whose names had been submitted by the British Embassy. I was informed that regular meetings were arranged with Gaddafi for British women who felt that they had been somehow victimised or treated unfairly while in Libya.

Vincent Fean called me beforehand, advising on what I should say. It was thoughtful of him, but I knew exactly what to say. We had arranged to meet at the British Embassy, but I had been warned that Colonel Gaddafi often kept people waiting for hours on end so I had no idea when the meeting would actually take place. Half an hour later, however, two large limousines pulled up and I climbed onto the back seat of one of them.

We were taken to a secret location, which appeared to be an army barracks. After being instructed to leave our bags and mobile phones in the cars, we went through a metal detector machine – the sort they have at airports. We were then led down some stairs and into a small underground room full of comfy mendars. There, we made ourselves comfortable and a man in a white suit came into the room. After introducing himself as Nuri Al-Mismari, the Head of Protocol, he told us that the Leader was on his way but first wanted to hear my story.

I explained everything to him. He was amazed and told me that he would explain it all to Colonel Gaddafi. We were then served with drinks, sweets and various confectionaries. I helped myself to a cake and turned around to return to my seat when there, standing right in front of me, was the Leader! It was as if he had appeared from nowhere. I stared at him long and hard – I couldn't believe that this infamous man was so close to me. He was smaller than I had imagined and wearing a floral shirt and beige slacks; his hair was tousled and he looked a bit dishevelled, like he had just got out of bed. He shook all our hands and welcomed us. Nuri Al-Mismari spoke to him in Arabic and Gaddafi responded by pointing to a telephone on the other side of the room. About six of his lackeys dived for it, each one eager to please their master.

Gaddafi made a call – and to this day I don't know who to – and he kept repeating the Arabic word for 'now'. I could only pray that he was ordering someone to find Nadia immediately. I felt elated – I knew how powerful the Libyan President was; no one would disobey his orders. Although, by all accounts, he could speak English quite well, he would only speak in Arabic. Through the Head of Protocol, Gaddafi assured me that Nadia would be 'sleeping at my side by midnight tonight'. I then spoke to the Leader myself and explained that I would do anything for my daughter – I even said I would live in the middle of the desert, if I had to! I just wanted her back. Gaddafi simply nodded his head but didn't say anything.

We said our farewells and then Nuri took us to his office and issued instructions to the police to find – and arrest – Fawzi. He was still refusing to divulge Nadia's whereabouts but he was flouting the court so he could now be held and questioned. Every time Nuri's telephone rang while we were there, I was onto him like a flash, asking who was on the phone. This guy is one of the highest-ranking officials in Libya and there I was, demanding to know who was calling him! Nuri allowed me to ring Mum from his office to tell her about the meeting with Gaddafi and let her know that I should have Nadia by the end of the evening. Naturally, she was ecstatic about the news.

Nuri then informed us that, on Colonel Gaddafi's orders, he had invited us all to dinner. Although the Leader wouldn't be there, Nuri would represent him. We were taken to the city's zoo, of all places, where there was a VIP lounge, which was built for and catered to the whims of Gaddafi and his close associates. There, we were treated to vodka from Nuri's private stock and a five-course meal with wine. During the feast, Nuri's phone rang. *Could this be the call I was waiting for?* It wasn't. The call was, in fact, to inform Nuri that my ex-husband had been arrested. Nadia hadn't been with him, and he was refusing to say where she was, or to give up any information. I was in tears – I was so certain that I was going to have Nadia back, just as Colonel Gaddafi had promised. After the dinner, I went home but was unable to settle, constantly looking at my watch as midnight approached and then passed. I wouldn't have Nadia in my bed after all; even the much-feared dictator had failed to get her back.

A few weeks after I had seen Colonel Gaddafi, I was summoned to see the Court Prosecutor. He was a good-looking man, very tall and immediately sympathetic.

Arvinder Vohra accompanied me and told me that, on my way into the court, I would pass a cage where prisoners are kept and Fawzi might be in there. He added, if this was the case, I should ignore my ex-husband and just walk past. As I came to the top of the stairs, Fawzi was in the cage and looking straight at me. The pen was about three metres long and of a similar width – not very big at all, and there were about ten men in there. It was very hot and I can't imagine how they must all have felt, but I didn't feel sorry for them – they were criminals. Arvinder and the driver, Mohammed, waited around while I went inside to see the Prosecutor. Fawzi was refusing to give over any information, so I needed to inform the Prosecutor of all the people who might be hiding Nadia and any addresses of Fawzi's friends or family. As it was getting late, the Prosecutor asked me to return the following day.

The next day, Fawzi was still in the cage and looked even rougher. When I walked past him, he spat some Arabic words at me, one of which was prostitute. A guard told him to shut up or he would be slapped. I was interviewed through an interpreter by the Prosecutor; there was also a clerk, who wrote down everything that was said by hand; there wasn't a computer in sight. Around twenty minutes into the interview, I looked carefully at the scribe: there was something familiar about him and his presence was making me feel a bit uneasy. Suddenly, I realised the man was a friend of Fawzi's and had been one of his confederates at the meeting the day after my former husband had assaulted me.

I informed the interpreter and he told the Prosecutor, who slammed his pen down. The clerk was gob-smacked, but admitted that he knew Fawzi. He was ordered to stand up and hand over his ID card. The Prosecutor ripped up the pages that had already been written and told the clerk to leave. I think he may have sacked the clerk, who should have informed us that he knew Fawzi as he shouldn't have been involved in the case. I was just thankful that I had recognised him, otherwise all the information and my plans would have been given to Fawzi.

I was interviewed for three hours before the Prosecutor called Fawzi into the room. Fawzi sat down but was ordered to stand up. He did so reluctantly, but slouched with his hands in his pockets. The Prosecutor ordered him to stand up straight. He then asked him to co-operate and tell us where Nadia was being kept. Fawzi refused. Later, I found out that he had defiantly stated: 'You can bring the Leader here himself and put a gun to my head, but I'm not going to tell you where Nadia is.'

The authorities could only hold Fawzi in prison for up to three months and he then had to be released, even if he failed to tell the police where Nadia was being kept. She had also been taken out of her school to prevent the police from snatching her back. Vincent and his staff at the British Embassy requested the police to have Fawzi watched in order to find her, but this proved fruitless.

During the next few months, there were a number of court appearances due to Fawzi's claims, counterclaims and various appeals. He now stated, through his lawyer, that I was a prostitute, a drunk and a drug addict unable to provide Nadia with a safe and secure home but I never lost my temper and always remained calm when we appeared before the judge. I stuck to my guns about Fawzi's unreasonable behaviour and provided evidence as to all his wrongdoings.

On 28 September, Vincent Fean met with Nuri Al-Mismari to find out what was going on. He discovered that, after Fawzi's release, Fawzi's mother Mona and sister Mufeda were arrested and questioned, but were also released and no further information had been obtained. Nuri agreed to speak to the Leader again for assistance; he also agreed to telephone Fawzi himself to order him to hand Nadia over, while at the same time he assured him that she wouldn't be able to leave the country so he wouldn't be separated from her in the long term. I was gutted to hear this. By now, I knew that I couldn't possibly live in Libya permanently, even if I got Nadia back, but I also knew that I had to go along with the plan for the time being. I just hoped that, when Nuri did call Fawzi, he would be his usual arrogant self and prove exactly how impossible he was to deal with.

But I was never able to see Colonel Gaddafi again. I thought that for some reason Sana, who had been so helpful at the beginning, had now become obstructive and wasn't passing on the various messages. I wondered if the fact that his orders had not been carried out might be seen as her responsibility and she and her colleague were now covering their tracks.

I telephoned Mark Matthews, the newly appointed Assistant Ambassador at the Embassy, to see if he had heard anything from Nuri. He told me to be patient as Nuri was a very busy man, but he would get onto it. I was sick and tired of hearing the same old thing and no action being taken. Maybe I needed to come at this from another direction, perhaps take the law into my own hands and think about snatching Nadia back. During this period, I thought a lot about it. I could wear a burka, the sort of costume that only shows your eyes. I was even thinking of disguising myself by sticking a cushion under my top to make it look as if I was pregnant, and then walking past Fawzi's house and snatching Nadia back.

On 12 September, Mum and Dad had had an appointment to see Andy Burnham, the Labour MP for Leigh, our local Member of Parliament, who was also a Government Minister. Andy had heard about our story through the local press some time ago and had offered help, but at that time we thought making the case overtly political might be counterproductive. Now we were getting desperate and sought all the help we could. Mum and Dad poured out their hearts to him at his advice surgery and he was immediately moved by the story. He was amazed that I had already been to see Colonel Gaddafi, so he knew I meant business! Andy could identify with my desperate situation because he has daughters of his own; he had also been affected by the disappearance of three-year-old Madeleine McCann while on holiday in Portugal, just three weeks before Nadia was kidnapped.

Andy said he would do all he could to help and would begin by bringing it to the attention of the Foreign Secretary, David Miliband, and the then Prime Minister, Gordon Brown. Mum had rung me in an excited state to tell me all this and said she had been moved to tears by Andy's reaction. This was more like it! Andy Burnham knew all the right people in the right places and now world leaders were to be involved in Nadia's rescue.

Behind the scenes, Andy sprang into action; he got in touch with Detective Inspector Phil Owen and remained in touch throughout my ordeal in Libya. He also wrote to David Miliband, who was very interested and helpful, but wrote to Andy that the matter was in hand and that Vincent Fean, in his role as Ambassador, was doing all he could. However, David Miliband also wrote to the Libyan Foreign Minister, Abdul Rahman Shalgam, on 29 September, and Bill Rammell, Foreign & Commonwealth Office Minister for Libya, raised the case with the Libyan Minister for Europe, Abdul Ati al-Obeidi, when they met in London on 9 October.

Andy Burnham also went to see the Libyan chargé d'affaires in London, Omar Jelban. In fact, Andy told me later that Mr Jelban was always very helpful and sympathetic, and was convinced that I would get Nadia back, but it had to be when it suited the Libyan authorities. It would always be in the Libyans' own time, no matter what the weight of diplomatic pressure from the British Government. I'm not sure whether I would have wanted to know that at the time or not, but I do know that Andy's involvement did help in the end.

As I've already mentioned, Andy was in regular contact with Phil Owen. Phil was just incredible. Although he had been transferred to Manchester after I had moved to Libya, he requested permission to be able to stay involved in my case. Whenever I felt isolated or scared, I used Phil as my sounding board. I must have spoken to him at least once or twice a week while I was in Tripoli, but he never let me down or avoided talking to me. Once I even rang him during his holidays, when he was sailing down the Nile! He always listened patiently to my worries and responded to my many requests. Phil, in turn, received great support and assistance from the Child Abduction Section at the British Foreign & Commonwealth Office.

I'd been in Libya for about ten months when I found an adult education centre that required an English-speaking tutor to teach English language. The money wasn't brilliant because it was for just eight hours a week (120 dinars/£60 a week), but it meant that I had a little to spend on myself, and taxi fares to and from the court. They didn't ask for any previous teaching experience and I started straight away. The students were aged between sixteen and thirty, and were really nice and eager to learn. I enjoyed it there but, in the summer, Patricia – Nadia's old teacher – got in touch and said they were looking for teachers in her school. It would be strange working at the place where Nadia had been a pupil, but I decided to go and see the head teacher, Naja, and hear what she had to say.

The school was private and catered for both British and Libyan children. Naja asked if I had a CV. Without blinking, I told her that I did, but that it was in the UK – a complete bluff. I then exaggerated my teaching qualifications – well, when I say exaggerated, it was actually total fiction because I didn't have any! Anyway, it worked because they offered me the job, which was to start in the new autumn term, giving me about two weeks to wait.

Naja said the school employed drivers to chauffeur the teachers to and from school, so I wouldn't need to find money to pay for a taxi. The school day began at 8am and finished at 2pm, so these hours would give me time when I needed to go to the Embassy.

The day before I started, I went into the school to see what I needed to do to prepare myself. I was asked to teach children aged seven and eight, just a little older than Nadia, who was now six. I would have loved for Fawzi to have registered Nadia in the school again and seen his face when he saw me there! Sadly, it never happened. The school was off a main road and I had to walk down a dirt path similar to Fawzi's street, but much longer, to get there. Later on, I discovered that, when there was a lot of rain, the road flooded and it was sometimes hard to get down it.

The classrooms were really depressing; the walls were

bare and there were no teaching aids or even toys. I wondered how the children were meant to learn without anything to make it more fun. I decided to make my mark straight away and transformed the classroom by making it as bright, attractive and stimulating as possible; I was determined to decorate the walls with drawings and paintings. My classroom was upstairs and quite small for the thirty-five pupils for whom I was responsible. A pretty big-sized class when you come to think of it, especially for a complete novice like me! I also noticed there was no air conditioning, only an electric fan attached to the ceiling. Once all the pupils were in the classroom, it was very hot.

I was quite nervous on my first day and wasn't used to getting up at 6am. However, I soon discovered that the school was pretty basic and the kids were academically about a year behind the equivalent age back home. The children I taught were lovely, but some of the Libyan children were a bit naughty and so I had to lay down the law from the very beginning to make sure they knew who the boss was. I loved the work and got satisfaction out of doing my job. The kids were from well-off families and they all spoke English. There was another class with the same-aged pupils, so we worked together. Thank God my colleague was a qualified teacher! I learned a lot from her.

I was immediately struck by a girl in the class, a delightful little creature who reminded me of Nadia. Eager to know more about her, I asked her where she lived and the names of her mummy and daddy. It wasn't as if I thought she was Nadia, but perhaps finding out about her made me feel closer to my own little girl. My imagination played strange tricks on me during those dark days, but I did my best to keep the two girls separate in my mind.

No one at the school was aware of my story and I kept it that way for a while, until my colleagues began to get to know me. Patricia didn't mention my situation to anyone. Quite often, when I had a free lesson I would go and sit in her classroom and talk to her. Her husband was Libyan and all her children were married to Libyans. I still think about how kind she was to me during that period.

The only other teachers I spoke to were Joliette and her husband Henry, the Head of English. They were a lovely South African couple. Henry was always understanding about allowing me time off to go to court. I decided to go and see Henry to see if they still had Nadia's records. They did, and he showed me her reports – there wasn't much information that I didn't already know, although there was a passport picture of Nadia, which I kept. I made lots of copies and took them to the Embassy, so that they had a recent picture.

While teaching at the school, I got friendly with some of the families. At parents' evening, they told me that their children were enjoying my class and would go home and talk about the fun day they'd had at school. The parents stated how much their children had blossomed and how much their English had improved, although none of them learned any Wiganese! Having never done anything like teaching children before, I felt quite proud of myself.

One of the mothers, who had a boy in my class, was called Hanan. It turned out she was a lawyer. Her English was very good and, when she came to collect her son at the end of school, we would always have a chat. Coincidentally, at the same time, nothing much was happening in regard to the legal situation and I sensed Mohammed was beginning to back off a bit. He had been worried when Colonel Gaddafi became involved and he had become more distant. I felt more able to explain myself to Hanan – not only was her English better, but also she was a woman and more empathetic, and I felt I could express my thoughts and feelings to her more easily. More importantly, she was, after all, a mother like me.

I approached Hanan and asked if I could speak to her in confidence. She invited me to her house and I explained about Nadia. I liked her, felt very comfortable in her presence and, most importantly, I trusted her. She agreed to take over my case and I was delighted. Hanan contacted Mohammed, who I think was quite relieved and grateful to hand all the paperwork over to her.

Meanwhile, there was some lovely news from home in October 2008 when I became an auntie for the first time. Andy and Kirsty's daughter Frankie was born. I had known of Kirsty's pregnancy from early on and I was thrilled for them both. Funnily enough, I didn't feel a pang of jealousy that I had lost a daughter and Andy had been blessed with Frankie – just a sense of sadness that I couldn't be there to share their joy. Andy told me that, while this was one of the greatest days of his life, he still had an overbearing feeling of guilt. He explained later that he found it difficult to bond with his new daughter while I, his sister, was battling to see her own child. He was also worried if Mum and Dad would bond with a granddaughter in the same way. Very recently, he told me that he sometimes wished he lived away from Wigan, back then, because he didn't want the family thinking that Frankie was to be a replacement for Nadia. It was a really difficult situation for Andy and Kirsty, and something he has only just revealed to me, but I completely understand what he must have been going through. He knows now that Frankie wasn't going to replace Nadia and everybody loved Frankie for being Frankie.

When Mum and Dad visited me a couple of months later at Christmas, they brought pictures of my new niece. This was the first time Andy had been apart from our parents on Christmas Day, although of course he understood that they had to visit me. I wrote a letter to my new niece. The letter is still in Frankie's memory box; Andy and Kirsty read it occasionally as a reminder of what the family has been through. During their visit, Mum, Dad and I had a few meals out and they accompanied me to court a couple of times. We didn't do a great deal – we just wanted to be together.

By now, Hanan was representing me at the court hearings, which were held once or twice a month. I was either ringing or popping into the British Embassy to check for any news. At one stage, Arvinder suggested that I should go home to recharge my batteries for a week; he even offered to help with the fare from his own savings. But I couldn't go. Suppose I wasn't allowed back in the country? What if they found Nadia and I wasn't there? It would have felt like turning my back on her. Of course, it may have been because Arvinder had tired of my demands and this was actually an excuse to have a break from me!

Back at home, Andy Burnham, who was increasingly worried about the lack of progress, sent another letter to David Miliband in February 2009 stating that Phil Owen was willing to travel to Libya to work alongside the Libyan authorities and help track down Nadia; it would have been funded by the Greater Manchester Police. Although this sort of thing was normal practice between police forces of two EU Member States, there were obviously protocol issues but we hoped that the Libyans would be sympathetic. Bill Rammell also raised it several times with the Libyan Minister for Europe, Mr al-Obeidi. Unfortunately, the answer came back that the Libyan authorities wouldn't welcome such 'assistance' – they clearly felt this was outside interference and made it quite clear that they would not support a visa application from Phil. It was felt that any further pressure to try to obtain a visa for Phil might cause political embarrassment, and therefore could work against us. It was a real blow – not only would Phil, being a strong character, have got things moving but also, selfishly, it would have been brilliant to have him around to boost my spirits.

Fawzi was kept in jail for a month before being released with no explanation. He was imprisoned on several occasions but would never divulge where Nadia was. I heard that he had been beaten up by his captors, but had been released – they could only keep him for three months at a time. There were also a couple of court cases in May without any resolution. I was told that Fawzi's house was under constant police surveillance but there was still no sign of Nadia; she was obviously being moved around. I learned that there had even been a couple of raids on various members of Fawzi's family, but without success. Fawzi seemed to be one step ahead of the police at all times. My suspicion that there was an informer in the police department seemed prophetic: I had lost all faith in them and didn't think I could trust anyone in the force.

On 28 June 2009, Andy Burnham kept the promise he made to my parents and came out to see me. I had asked Mum to give him some more of the newspaper cuttings about Fawzi, so that he would be well prepared for his official meetings. Of course, this was an easy request for me to make, but Dad recently reminded me he had to go through over thirty boxes of my possessions to find what was required!

I'll never forget that Andy was so committed to my

cause and even funded the 24-hour trip himself. It was strange that he had had quite a lot of contact with my parents and he knew all about me, but until now we had never met. I greeted him at the Embassy, where he was to stay the night, and immediately liked him: warm and friendly, I felt that he was truly engaged in my situation. Andy arrived in quite an optimistic mood and believed that together we would achieve something positive. He got on well with Vincent, and the fact that we were all Lancastrians meant that we formed a bond, despite Vincent being a Burnley supporter and Andy a staunch Evertonian!

Andy said it was very unusual for an MP to undertake such a mission on constituency business, but he wanted to do all he could. I know he had even given up seeing his son play in his first-ever cricket match for me.

It had worked in our favour that a concordat in regard to healthcare had been signed with Libya, so there had been ongoing dialogue between our Department of Health and the Libyan Health Minister. Andy thought as an ordinary MP he wouldn't be granted a meeting to discuss Nadia, but as Health Minister he might be afforded more respect and thus able to negotiate with his Libyan counterpart. Although our situation had absolutely nothing to do with matters of health, Andy thought that he could use the auspices of health discussions to raise the subject of Nadia's kidnapping.

Andy and I discussed everything at length before going out for something to eat with Arvinder, Farouk and one of the security guys from the Embassy. I kept up the talk throughout dinner, so Andy was totally prepared for his meetings, due to take place the following morning. It was agreed that Arvinder, Farouk and I would all meet around midday at the Embassy, when he would report back on what had taken place. As planned, we met the following lunchtime: I was half-hoping that Andy would turn up then with Nadia, which of course didn't happen. I know I was being unrealistic, but I had to have my fantasies to keep my resolve.

Andy told us that, at the first gathering, he and Vincent had met with the Libyan Health Minister and, after talking about pertinent matters relating to the concordat, he suddenly brought up Nadia's kidnapping. They were a bit shocked, but reluctantly listened to what he had to say.

He then went on to meet with Abdul Ati al-Obeidi, once the Libyan Head of State, who held a position in the security services. It seems the atmosphere was pretty tense, and Andy felt that al-Obeidi and his men weren't giving him much attention until he produced the newspaper cuttings of Fawzi to show them that they were protecting a criminal. Andy threatened to file for Fawzi's extradition unless something was done to find Nadia. They were taken aback by this and seemed to take his warning seriously.

Andy also told al-Obeidi that Colonel Gaddafi and Prime Minister Gordon Brown were meeting at the G8 Summit in the near future and he was going to request Mr

Brown raise the subject of Nadia with the Leader and remind him that, despite his earlier intervention, nothing had been achieved. He thought this had been heeded and relayed what al-Obeidi had said about hearing something in the next few days. As much as I appreciated Andy's efforts, I didn't think I would hold my breath for some action – after all, I'd been told this many times before. Andy told me that he had continued to be in regular contact with Omar Jelban in London, who told him to be patient. 'Slowly, slowly' – I had heard this from so many people in Libya that I was beginning to get sick of the words. Things had gone 'slowly, slowly' enough!

We had lunch at Vincent's and, when it was time for Andy to leave, he gave me a warm hug and told me that he wasn't going to let things go, he was very much involved and intended to continue doing all he could. I know that, despite his outward optimism, Andy left Tripoli feeling quite despondent and, although he tried to put on a brave face in order to protect me, I felt equally pessimistic.

A couple of weeks later, Vincent rang to tell me that he had been advised that Nadia had been seen by the Libyan police in a Union Jack dress. I thought that this was absolutely ridiculous; there is no way on this earth that Fawzi would dress Nadia in such attire – it would be like advertising to the world where she was. Apparently the secret police, the Libya External Security Organisation (ESO), had followed her into a shop but then lost her. I didn't believe it, and wondered whether they were concocting a story just to make me think they were doing something. Now that Andy Burnham was putting some pressure on them, they needed to be seen to be active.

From then on, I began to lose all faith in their activities. Worse still, for the first time I feared for Nadia's safety. She hadn't been seen for over a year, and there was no evidence that she was still alive. I had already thought about whether Fawzi or his family would actually harm her and the terrible possibility of an honour killing. Nadia was completely blameless in this matter and I couldn't believe that anything terrible might have befallen her, but the more time that elapsed without me seeing her only added to my fears. I tried to put these thoughts out of my head – I had to believe that, whatever her situation, Nadia was being looked after and we would one day be reunited.

Another court hearing was held on 9 July 2009, which I attended with Arvinder, Farouk and Hanan, my lawyer. This time, Fawzi, casually dressed in jeans and a green linen T-shirt, didn't have any legal representation. He was then joined by a friend, whom I had never seen before who seemed to be acting as a character witness. Fawzi showed this man some pictures of Nadia on his phone. He made sure I knew what he was doing, and I could only guess the sole reason was to upset me and gauge my reaction. How evil could he get?

When we were called, I produced the newspaper cuttings and the police evidence of his alleged crimes. Fawzi was shocked. I also handed my passport to the judge to prove I wasn't in the country illegally, as this was another of Fawzi's accusations. Fawzi attempted to tell the judge that I was travelling on an illegal passport and my visa was invalid, but he failed miserably. He couldn't get his words out and was stuttering so much that the judge asked us to take a break. When we resumed, Fawzi was fuming and announced that he had received a phone call from his family, telling him that the police had been to his house to find Nadia. He said that he had advised his family members to give the police some money and the police had subsequently gone away. All this was said in Arabic and my lawyer translated. Even though Fawzi seemed to be admitting bribery, the judge took no notice. It seemed that Fawzi was talking nonsense, purely out of bravado, about how he could get away with anything.

It really wound me up, which was probably the other reason why Fawzi invented this tale and fake telephone call. He made no eye contact with me at all the whole time we were in the courtroom. Once again, the case was adjourned as Fawzi's lawyer hadn't turned up – he was ill, according to Fawzi. The nameless witness had also disappeared and obviously wasn't returning.

The following day was my birthday and a much better day all round – the G8 Summit was being held in Italy and I'd been promised my case would be discussed. The politicians stayed in a converted police barracks block, but Colonel Gaddafi stayed in a pitched tent in the grounds of the summit site, overseen by his all-female personal bodyguard in blue and gold uniforms.

At one stage during the proceedings, Gaddafi and Prime Minister Gordon Brown had a private 45-minute meeting during which they discussed Libya's call for the return of the Lockerbie bomber (Abdelbaset Ali Mohmed al-Megrahi) and the case of WPC Yvonne Fletcher, shot dead outside Libya's London Embassy in 1984. They also talked about Nadia, and afterwards a Downing Street spokesman said that Colonel Gaddafi had 'promised to consider Mr Brown's request that Nadia be returned to Britain'.

Mum rang to tell me that she had heard the news on the radio and I had also been featured on the *News at Ten*. Phil Owen also called to advise me that the meeting had been reported in all the newspapers. There was further contact from Andy Burnham, who confirmed that the Prime Minister had raised the issue and Gaddafi had replied that he would do all he could to help resolve the situation as soon as possible. Andy was very confident that something positive would come out of their discussion and I was excited: if I needed further pressure from powerful men, surely I couldn't do much better than Brown and Gaddafi!

Mum, Dad and the whole family were asked to give statements to the press, but I told them to refuse. I didn't want the press to be involved because the coverage might upset the Libyan authorities and disrupt any high-level negotiations.

Phil called me and asked if I wanted to speak to a child psychologist about Nadia. He felt that, when we were reunited, it might help to have some hints and techniques about how to try to help Nadia cope with yet another big change in her life. I agreed to this sensible suggestion and it was a bit of a boost to plan for that day, even though I had no idea when it might happen.

A woman called Lynn Clark, who Phil knew through his professional contacts, duly rang me. We had a long chat and she was incredibly sympathetic and reassuring. Apparently, I was already doing the right thing in bringing with me Nadia's old toys, photographs of the family and pieces that would remind her of home when we finally met. Lynn also explained that I shouldn't expect too much from Nadia at first and to try not to overwhelm her; I should try to react to Nadia's mood and take my cues from her behaviour. This was all very helpful because I knew it would be difficult for me not to go over the top. Lynn refused any payment for her services – another fantastic gesture.

Andy Burnham rang again and we discussed my disappointment that nothing had transpired following the meeting between the Leader and the Prime Minister three weeks earlier. There were a couple of things that I wanted Andy to do for me: I asked if he could contact Gordon Brown and request him to give the Leader a courtesy call. I also wanted Nadia to be deemed a 'missing person' as it was now obvious that the Libyan authorities had no idea where she was. He promised to do what he could. In retrospect, it is interesting to note even then, some time before the revolution that eventually toppled Colonel Gaddafi, the Leader didn't have absolute power in his country – otherwise he would have secured Nadia for me. Obviously, there were already factions working against him.

In August 2009, I moved into my own accommodation, a rather shabby flat in a small apartment block. I'd been dependent on Sally and her family for long enough. I have to admit I was a bit scared about being on my own and having to live independently – I only knew a few words of Arabic. I felt isolated and frightened, but my obsession with rescuing Nadia kept me going. Two birthdays and Christmases had dragged by without her. For each occasion we should have been celebrating together, I had bought her cards and presents, hoping one day I'd be able to give them to her. I was so scared that Nadia might forget who I was; not being able to see her was torture.

Soon after I moved into my new rented accommodation in Tripoli, my own house in Wigan was repossessed. After leaving England, I had received some pay from my work for the first few months and had kept up the mortgage payments but, as time went by, I could no longer keep up the instalments. Mum had attempted to sell the house and had almost agreed the sale when we had a surprising offer from Donya: she said she wanted to buy the property and then rent it to me when I returned from Libya.

Mum and Dad shelled out for some legal costs for me, but, after a few weeks of negotiation with her solicitor, Donya pulled out. We never found out why. The house was repossessed and I told Mum and Dad to sell any furniture they could and send me the money. It was a sad time, as this was the home that Nadia and I had last shared, but in the end it was only bricks and mortar: the things that really mattered were my family and getting Nadia back.

I had been working at the school for nearly an academic year, but, in the summer of 2009, I left. By then, I was struggling for money – there were more court appearances, which I needed to pay for. One of Sally's friends helped find me a full-time job as a secretary for Samsung. I went into the school at the beginning of the new autumn term to collect my belongings and I'd bought a big bag of sweets for my class. As soon as the children saw me, they all came running out to greet and hug me. I felt very emotional and I was so glad that I'd had the opportunity to work with such lovely kids. It was like the scene in *Kindergarten Cop*, where Mr Kimble goes back to see the children – the only difference was I didn't have a broken leg and I suppose I'm not really like Arnold Schwarzenegger, apart from longing for 'Judgment Day'!

CHAPTER 8

False Trails, Videos and a Yashmak

Between August and December 2009, I kept an occasional journal, which began with a much-anticipated visit from my parents:

20 August 2009

Mum and Dad finally arrived after trouble with their visas. [Andy Burnham actually helped them sort this out with the Libyan authorities.] It was wonderful to have them here; they give me so much support. They told me a story which cheered me up. On their way to Manchester Airport the taxi driver asked them where they were going, and when they told him that they were coming to Libya, the cabbie was reminded of our story. He refused to take any money for the fare and asked Dad to give the money to Nadia's charity. It's the sort of generosity and kindness which has typified how people have been to me during this whole terrible experience.

27 August 2009

Due in court today – glad Mum and Dad are here to see what it's like and what I have to go through almost every other week. Hopefully, their presence will put a little more pressure on Fawzi, too. I had been told a couple of days ago that something might come out of today's appearance but I must stay calm. Farouk and Arvinder are both coming along.

We had a call, advising us that the hearing will start at 10am rather than the usual 9am, so we decided to go to the Embassy and wait there for a while. We arrived at the courthouse to see Hanan and Fawzi leaving. I was gutted. Hanan told me that the case had been heard at 9am after all. This was the first time I had missed a hearing in nearly two years. I promise it will also be the last time I do this – I feel I've let us down, not being there for Nadia.

Farouk made a few calls and told me that Fawzi has been arrested again. I was surprised; I hadn't seen many police around. Farouk said he would make enquiries and find out what's happened. I have mixed feelings about Fawzi being arrested. It doesn't seem to matter how long he is in prison, he just won't let on where Nadia is. At least if he's on the outside he can be watched, although nothing has been achieved by that method either. I harangued Arvinder and Farouk all weekend to see what happened in court, but no one seems to know, other than the fact that the case was adjourned for what seems like the 100th time because Fawzi has a personal witness, who has agreed to testify against me.

2 September 2009

Mum and Dad have had a lovely time. I'm just so sorry they couldn't see Nadia in the last fortnight while they were here, but I can't show them how upset I am – I don't want them to worry.

After a tearful farewell at the airport, I went straight to the Embassy. Luckily, Farouk was there with Anne and Walid, Vincent's driver. I asked again what had happened in court a week ago, but Farouk wasn't clear. I started to get upset and told him that I had just seen my parents off at the airport and that we were all in floods of tears because no progress is being made. And no one can tell me what's going on. Farouk made some more calls and was told that Fawzi had been taken yesterday to see Mr al-Obeidi, one of the police chiefs. I don't know what came of the meeting and I'm not sure it's even true. Yesterday was the 40th anniversary of Gaddafi's coup, and I'm sure al-Obeidi would have been very busy with the anniversary.

I loved having Mum and Dad here, but I hate having to see them off and not knowing when I'll see them again. I feel particularly miserable this time. I need to be alone for a while.

10 September 2009

Didn't spend much time with the girls this week; I needed some space and wanted to be on my own for a while.

Another court appearance today and Fawzi arrived, obviously released from prison, looking like The Sheik of Araby. He's grown a beard. He was wearing a long white gown and a black taqiyah [a rounded cap worn by devout Muslims]. What's he doing? He is so pathetic, trying to present himself as the respectable pious father. Everyone can see right through him. To my surprise, Brian turned up with Fawzi. He'd told me previously that he'd had a big fight with Fawzi and that he thought Fawzi had behaved badly and was in the wrong, so what's he doing here now? He's just like a lapdog. If he's the character witness, then I don't have anything to worry about as I know him well, and he has nothing on me. Brian would soon be discredited if he tried to lie.

We stood outside for a while, waiting for the judge to arrive. Five police officers entered the courthouse and one of them shook Farouk's hand and asked where Fawzi was. A few minutes later, Fawzi was brought out of the waiting room, grabbed by the police and taken away. His lawyer, Brian and his brother were still inside the courtroom. We went into the courtroom and Fawzi returned, escorted by the police officers. They were watching him like hawks.

Fawzi spat some insult at me and was giving me the evil eye all the time. He produced a phone from his pocket and took pictures of me and Arvinder. We told Hanan, who spoke to Fawzi's lawyer, and Fawzi was told to delete the pictures.

Brian and another guy came in. I'd never seen this other man, and, when the judge asked to see ID, he wasn't able to produce any documentation and was ordered out of the court. Brian then proceeded to give evidence and stated, 'I've heard Sarah's a drunk and I've heard Sarah sleeps around.' But this was all hearsay evidence and not admissible. Fawzi also said that I had changed my religion – all rubbish, of course – he was just trying to delay things. And he succeeded because the case was adjourned for another two weeks.

Fawzi was taken away again by the police. Arrested again for not obeying the court's order to divulge Nadia's whereabouts.

11 September 2009

Heard from home today; my old school friend, Kelly, and her husband, Dave, arranged a fund-raising auction and party at the local rugby club.

Amongst other 'lots', my cousin Simon had managed to get hold of a pair of Amir Khan's boxing gloves and a Manchester United shirt, signed by Ryan Giggs. Local boxer and British champion Michael Jennings also contributed some gloves and tickets to his next bout.

I had written a speech for them to deliver at the event, thanking everyone for their support. I'd started with the following:

I just want to thank everyone for coming and I wish I was there with you all. I'm still here, fighting for my little girl, Nadia, and I've no intention of giving up. She's my life and I need her with me. I still can't believe how much support I'm still getting from you lot. It is things like this 'do' tonight that keep me going, knowing I've got so much support and love from family and friends. I'm overwhelmed.

Apparently, Dave tried to deliver my speech, but started crying and couldn't continue. Jay, Steph's boyfriend, then tried to read it out, but then he was overcome. Then my dad tried, and he broke down. Three big strapping guys – all in tears! Eventually, they all read little bits of the speech between them and managed to get the words out.

24 September 2009

In court again. Fawzi didn't turn up, he's still in

prison, but all four of his brothers (Hakem, Hamdi, Fward and Ezzideen) turned up to intimidate me. Fat chance! The case has been adjourned for another week, but I was told that the judge gave Fawzi's lawyer a hard time and told her that, if she doesn't have any more evidence next week, his appeals will no longer be heard.

It's all very difficult to follow as the proceedings are conducted in Arabic, so I'm getting all the information second-hand, which is very frustrating at times. I only get to know what is said after we have left the courtroom. I'm not able to have my say as much as I'd like. Mind you, that's probably not such a bad thing – if I heard exactly what Fawzi was saying about me, I would probably have kicked off.

This is really getting to me now as at the last three court hearings I've been told that Fawzi's case will be dismissed, but it hasn't.

25 September 2009

Called Andy Burnham today and left a message on his answer-phone. I also sent Vincent a text message, asking if he could call me. I'm getting really anxious because Fawzi has now appealed to the High Court. I'm due to appear in ten days' time. He's now saying that we married in a mosque and that I had converted from the Church of England to become a Muslim and we haven't been divorced; I am therefore still married to him. This would affect the custody order. All lies. He can just make anything up, but doesn't seem to have to produce any evidence. The onus is always on me to provide proof to counter his malicious accusations. I will have to get Mum and Dad to go to the local mosque and get something in writing that we weren't married there. Unbelievable.

Fawzi's really getting desperate now, but I'm worried the longer this drags on, the longer he will have to think up more lies against me. This country is very corrupt: if you want something, and you have the money, you can procure any necessary paperwork. I really need the police to put real pressure on Fawzi to make him speak.

Andy called me back. He said there's a lot of political pressure going on at home, but he's trying to keep me out of the limelight because the press are trying to connect me with Abdelbaset al-Megrahi, the Lockerbie bomber. Andy was clear that they don't want me involved in some sort of deal in getting Nadia back if the British Government released Megrahi. Andy said he will call Jelban to see if he can find out anything else.

Vincent rang. He has a meeting with al-Obeidi next week. I really don't know what to expect any more. I'm getting so desperate and feeling really worn out. I am physically shattered and exhausted. I don't know how much more of this shit I can take from Fawzi any more, I'm afraid I may do something I'll regret. It has even crossed my mind to kidnap one of the other children in the family to see how they feel about having a child taken.

30 September 2009

What I wasn't fully aware of was that, behind the scenes, there are quite a lot of political negotiations taking place. Today Vincent met with the Justice Minister, Mustafa Mohammad Abdul Jalil, who stressed Libya's commitment to enforcing the court order and trying to reunite Nadia and me. He told Vincent he was sympathetic to my situation and would do whatever he could to ensure his Ministry's assistance. He also said that Fawzi would be prosecuted for 'the ongoing crime' and for 'violating the rule of law'. Jalil then mentioned that staff at border crossings had been alerted in case Fawzi attempted to take Nadia out of the country. He also stressed to Vincent that Libyan law states that a daughter cannot leave the country without the permission of the father, or of the court. Jalil concluded that the External Security Organisation (Libyan secret police) might be best placed to find Nadia.

[It is interesting to note that Abdul Jalil later resigned as Libya's Justice Minister after witnessing the shooting of peaceful demonstrators in the uprising against Colonel Gaddafi. He later became Head of State in the caretaker government.]

1 October 2009

In court today. Fawzi turned up with two police officers. He came out with the same old shit about me being sick. He produced a letter from a hospital here with information about the reoccurrence of leukaemia, but I have already produced medical evidence that states I'm fit and well. He was taken back to prison. The case was adjourned again for another three weeks, but I was told that the verdict will definitely be delivered that day. This means that Fawzi cannot produce any more lies to delay matters. Farouk told me that Fawzi will remain in prison until he gives up Nadia. The authorities have also threatened to arrest his brothers and family. The ESO have three locations where they think Nadia could be: the family home in Tripoli and two other places in Gharyan, a mountain town about sixty miles from Tripoli. They have all three locations under surveillance. I'm not sure what to think. Are they just telling me this to keep quiet? Why don't they just raid the three houses?

3 October 2009

An unexpected court appearance today. Fawzi has made yet another appeal – this time to the High Court, which I didn't know he could do. I can't believe it, especially after what I had been told just two days ago. He had a different lawyer representing him – apparently the head of the law firm. My dear friend and lawyer Hanan told me that he was very well known in Tripoli as one of the top lawyers. Fawzi is now saying that the custody order doesn't have his full name on it and is therefore invalid. We have to return in two weeks' time. Both Farouk and Hanan told me not to worry. Where have I heard that before?

4 October 2009

Farouk has spoken with Brigadier Gargoum (Director-General of Judicial Police), who says that's there's been 'no movement' at the three locations, but 'there will be something happening very soon' and I'm just to 'wait a little longer'. I seem to hang onto every word that I'm being told at the moment and try to be positive, but, on the other hand, this whole nightmare just drags on. I need to try and learn not to build my hopes up. Wait and see, as per usual.

17 October 2009

Arrived at the High Court. No sign of Fawzi and his lawyer. This could be because Fawzi has run out of money to pay the legal fees. He has had a number of lawyers over the last two years. He's probably engaging them, they take on the case and then they find out he can't pay them. Hanan also thinks that Fawzi has no funds left. There are three judges presiding at the High Court, so we have to convince all three of them that I'm in the right. Hanan did a brilliant job and definitely knows her stuff. The judges stated that Fawzi wouldn't be able to appeal again and produced relevant documentation. Hanan told me afterwards that she felt all three judges were sympathetic, and they told her that she was an excellent lawyer and had represented me very well. Although this was considered to be the highest court in the land, the setting was pretty shabby and the three judges – male, of course – were in ordinary clothes and seemed to spend a lot of time smoking and drinking tea.

21 October 2009

An appointment has been made for me to see al-Obeidi and I have prepared some of the points I want to raise with him.

First, I will say I am so grateful for his time.

I am concerned now for Nadia's welfare.

I have stuck entirely to the law. Fawzi has broken it all the time and is getting away with everything. Why?

I was willing to sign an agreement to bring Nadia up as Muslim, but Fawzi refused. I am still willing to sign that agreement.

What searches have they done?

Have they seen Nadia?

Arvinder told me today that some man has been

ringing the Embassy and was asking for me. He spoke to Joyce, a lady who worked alongside Arvinder in the Consular section, but wouldn't leave his name and he said he would call back.

22 October 2009

The verdict in the High Court was given today – in my favour. This is final. Fawzi has no more appeals. This is it, maybe…

24 October 2009

Met with Abdul Ati al-Obeidi today. Vincent and Arvinder accompanied me. The high-ranking officer had prepared for my visit, but didn't tell me anything I didn't already know. I became very angry and started shouting at him: 'Where is my daughter? Why can't you find her? Why don't you do something?' He admitted he didn't know. I asked him what they had been doing for the last six months.

Al-Obeidi agreed that Fawzi was a criminal and that his department was also concerned for Nadia's welfare. This admission made me feel even worse because this was the first time the authorities had expressed concern for Nadia. He could see I was upset and made a phone call to a man called Ajah to discuss what action they should take next.

Another call from Arvinder. The same man who had been trying to get hold of me earlier in the week had contacted the Embassy again and had spoken to Joyce. He had asked for my telephone number, which Joyce refused. He then asked for Joyce's number, which again she refused. He wanted her to arrange a private meeting with me. Joyce told him to call back tomorrow and she would make sure that I was at the Embassy to receive his call. He refused to say what he wanted to talk to me about. He was Libyan and couldn't speak English. I wondered why he would want my number if he couldn't speak English.

25 October 2009

I went to the Embassy at 2pm, the time the man said he would call back. He rang at 2.15pm. He spoke to Joyce and told her he knew where Nadia was. He said that she was being shifted between two houses. This makes sense as that's what one of the Libyan policemen had thought. Joyce asked him why he was doing this and who he was. When Joyce fired these questions at him, the man tried to change the subject. He said he wanted to keep his name out of the discussions and remain anonymous. Joyce assured him that whatever he said to the Embassy staff, or to me, would be kept confidential. He said he would call back in fifteen minutes when Joyce had had the opportunity to talk to me about what he had said.

I have no idea if he knows where Nadia is, or if there is any truth in what he is saying. On the other hand, he definitely knows that I'm at the Embassy, so I'm a little concerned that he could wait outside and even follow me home. The man called back at 2.55pm and asked Joyce if she had spoken to me. Joyce asked him to tell us where the two houses were and what else he knew. He refused to divulge the locations and was reluctant to give any information to her questions. He admitted that he had seen the story about Nadia on the internet and asked if I was going to put up a reward for getting her back.

I said that I hadn't offered a reward and so he said he wanted 1,500 dinars, the equivalent of approximately £750. He told me that I would get Nadia back if I agreed to meet him and hand over the money. I told him, via Joyce, that I would need time to raise the money and that he should ring again tomorrow.

Now he is talking about money, I'm getting more suspicious. All the information about Nadia on the internet is in English, and this man definitely doesn't speak English. I don't know what to do or think at the moment. Yet again, I'm very confused. This stranger might know something, and I can't afford to let an opportunity slip through my fingers. Or could Fawzi be behind it all? Is this a set-up?

I talked it over with the Embassy staff. They are very wary. First of all, they are concerned for my safety. Secondly, this could be seen as a bribe. If someone took a photo of me handing over money, it could be seen as me trying to subvert the justice system. I could be arrested, and I could join Fawzi in jail.

I really don't know what to do. I phoned Andy Burnham earlier in a very distressed state, crying down the phone, wanting his advice. He was really sympathetic, but it was difficult for him to give me a definitive 'Yes' or 'No' on this one. He could understand that I was very tempted to pay this stranger, but was equally concerned of the consequences if it was a sting. I also rang Phil Owen for advice, and he was very doubtful about the whole thing. I've been thinking long and hard about what to do and I'm beginning to wonder if this is one of Fawzi's brothers attempting a last-gasp effort to get me into trouble.

[In the end, after a sleepless night, going through all the pros and cons, I decided to continue working with the Libyan police and go through the diplomatic channels. I just hoped I was making the right decision and hadn't blown an opportunity to get Nadia back.]

19 November 2009

I had a call yesterday: al-Obeidi wants me to attend a meeting and bring a picture of Nadia. I'm worried as I don't know what to expect.

Arvinder, Mark (Assistant Ambassador) and I

went to al-Obeidi's office. It was only when we arrived that Arvinder told me that they have images of a little girl they think is Nadia, and they want me to identify her. I nearly fainted. My immediate reaction was that Nadia is alive: 'Please tell me it's true. Tell me it's her, please tell me!' Arvinder couldn't confirm it was her and said that all he had been told was that they have video footage of a girl they believe to be Nadia.

We arrived at al-Obeidi's building, where the ESO people were waiting for me. They confirmed that they had pictures of a little girl they believe to be Nadia. My eyes immediately went to the computer screen and I steeled myself. I looked at the pictures, but was immediately disappointed. The images were far too blurred to tell if it was Nadia or not. They started the download again. I stared intently, but I just couldn't tell. My gut feeling was that it wasn't Nadia, but I really wasn't sure.

The girl had been filmed coming out of a school, so I said I was willing to go there and see if I could see her. I said I would do this secretly and wear a traditional Muslim hijab or a yashmak so that I wouldn't be recognised. There was some discussion between them and al-Obeidi, and his men nodded in agreement. They told me the girl comes out of school at 1.30pm and I should meet Farouk at a restaurant near my flat at 1pm.

I went home all excited. Although I wasn't

convinced this was Nadia, there was a chance it was her and at least there was some action, which showed that the ESO are doing something at last. I changed into a long black dress and put a yashmak in my bag, which I could use to veil my face. I didn't want to be seen coming out of my flat wearing all this gear because it would look far too suspicious and draw attention to me. I have my suspicions that I'm being watched by the owner of the fruit and vegetable shop, who lives below my flat. He seems far too interested in my comings and goings.

At 1.15pm, I got a call from Farouk, who was outside the restaurant. I went there immediately and we hailed a taxi. Two minutes later, we stopped at a roundabout and got into the back of an unmarked police car, which was occupied by a plain-clothes female police officer and one of the External Security Agents, Ajah, I recognised from al-Obeidi's office. We arrived at the school and Ajah got out of the car, while the police officer and I moved into the front seats.

I saw Ajah cross the busy road and climb into a taxi that was parked on the other side of the road. It was only later that I learned that this taxi was actually another unmarked police car and the occupants were keeping their eyes on the school. The police officer didn't speak much English but tried to explain to me that the girl always went home in a school bus. The bus was usually parked outside the school, but today was stationed inside the school gates. She explained that, although this was more difficult, we would follow the bus when it left the school grounds.

There were a few phone calls between the police officer and Ajah, who could see the car park from where he was and would advise us of any movement. After a few minutes, the school bus exited the gates and we followed it, as planned. I realised with a bit of a shock that the vehicle was going in the direction of Fawzi's house. Perhaps Nadia was on the bus! It was very hard to see through the windows. There were about ten children on board and, if I was going to identify her, I would have to be quick. The bus stopped for the first time and a child got off. It wasn't Nadia. We drove past slowly and I tried to look inside at the other passengers.

As I scrutinised the bus, we were suddenly immersed in sunlight and my view was totally obliterated by the bright glare. I couldn't see a thing; I'd missed my opportunity. We pulled over and the bus drove past. It suddenly did a surprisingly quick U-turn and, before we had time to follow, a taxi came out of nowhere and the driver beckoned me to get in. We set off after the bus. Although the exterior of the vehicle looked just like a cab, the interior was full of CB radios, aerials and communication equipment.

The bus was definitely going in the direction of

Fawzi's house. I began to feel nervous and excited. After a few minutes, the bus came to a halt and a little girl got off outside a house in the street next to Fawzi's home. The taxi slowed down and I managed to take a look at the little girl. It wasn't Nadia; at least I didn't think so. The driver stared at me expectantly, I shook my head and then the driver sped away. Then I started to have some doubts. Could it have been her? What if she had changed that much that I didn't recognise her and it really was Nadia? I might have just thrown away my only chance of getting my daughter back. Could I have been so close to her and yet so far away? I was devastated and felt so foolish; I can't even recognise my own daughter now. I've let her down again. Oh God, I don't know anything any more.

I was taken back to the Embassy and I shamefacedly informed Farouk and Arvinder what had happened. I felt totally, completely shattered and confused. They tried to reassure me and said it was very difficult when I hadn't seen Nadia for so long. That gave me an idea: I wondered if someone could do a computer-generated image of Nadia as she might look now – like they had done for Maddie McCann. Nadia's face would have aged and having an up-to-date photo of her was bound to help. I need to keep up the momentum now that the police are finally taking some action. I must make sure that they have no excuse to slack off!

Phil Owen was the obvious person to call. I immediately had his full support for the idea. I knew I could rely on him and he sprang into action straight away. He asked me to email more photographs of Nadia, snaps of Fawzi and even images of me when I was Nadia's age. I rang Mum and she said she would sort them out and send them on to Phil. Despite the bitter disappointment that I had felt earlier in the day, I now feel more optimistic – I'm always better when I have a plan.

24 November 2009

The BBC have been in touch with Mum and Dad because the producers of *Inside Out*, a regional news show, want to do a piece about Nadia. They have discussed it with Phil Owen, who initially wasn't sure it was good idea (in case they try to sensationalise our story). He agreed to meet the producer, Sally Williams, anyway. Phil was impressed by her empathy and enthusiasm, and felt a television feature might help. I spoke to Sally, who suggested I record some sort of video diary. I think it's a really good idea to record my personal experiences and it will give me a focus.

I started recording some of my thoughts and described what's been going on. I obviously decided not to report any of the Libyan police activity, which has to remain secret. I found it a bit difficult to keep that part separate, but I reported on my court hearings and how I was feeling. I filmed myself in my flat and in front of the wall, which was festooned with photos of Nadia and old Christmas and birthday cards, and messages from home. I filmed all the toys and things I brought for Nadia. I also filmed lots of the places I had been since I moved to Tripoli. Some of my friends out here agreed to appear on the video and said what they thought about the situation. I think having the vocal support and character witnesses of as many people as possible will show the Libyans what type of person I am.

28 November 2009

I have finished my video diary and just hope it's the sort of thing they are looking for. I've never done anything like this before, and I've tried to make it as personal as possible. I've made sure everyone at home knows I'm never going to give up fighting for Nadia. Anyway, I did my best. I had to track all over Tripoli to find a FedEx to send it, helped by my friend Mohmed [a local shop owner], who found out where I had to go and gave a taxi driver exact directions.

After I sent the footage off, I went with a friend and her daughter to a shopping centre, called Souk lat. It's like a mini Trafford Centre. There's a supermarket there that we call 'Tesco' – it sells decent food, although it's not as well stocked as its British counterpart.

There are clothes shops, too, including Naf Naf and H&M, a few electrical shops and upstairs there is a food hall. We quite often have lunch here; it's much cheaper than England! Four dinars (£2) for a huge chicken sandwich meal with chips and a drink. With all that is going on, it was nice to do something that seemed normal and girly.

3 December 2009

Phil Owen has put me in touch with a woman called Teri, who will be doing Nadia's computerised aging process. She explained that she would try to merge a photograph of me when I was six years old into Nadia's picture, when she was four. Teri has promised to get back to me tomorrow with the first image.

4 December 2009

Teri did get back to me, as promised, and emailed me the first image. I was shocked at first, as Nadia looked as if she hadn't changed very much. I knew this wasn't a real picture of her, but I became quite emotional. In this image, Nadia looked so much like Mum – something that everyone used to say. Now, to see this photo in front of me was overwhelming. I also felt a little relieved – Nadia still looked like Nadia, and hadn't changed. I emailed my response to Teri and asked if she was sure that this was how Nadia would look. Of course, that was a bit silly as it was all computer-generated, but I was worrying that, if it wasn't accurate, then Nadia might have changed and I wouldn't be able to recognise her. Like everything else, it's all a bit confusing. Teri replied that it's not very likely that Nadia has changed that much and I would still recognise her. This did reassure me and I'm now sure that the little girl I saw a few weeks previous wasn't Nadia.

Teri sent me the final impression of Nadia, and I was moved to tears again; more relieved than anything, as she still looked very much the same.

5 December 2009

Met Arvinder and handed him the pictures. He wasn't so sure that Nadia looked a typical six-year-old. I wasn't bothered because I was satisfied more than anything that it still looked similar to Nadia, and that was the important thing.

[In fact, I later discovered that the computer-generated images weren't a particularly true likeness because Nadia had been living for almost two years in a completely different culture from what she had been used to. Apparently, climate, food and other variations in her lifestyle needed to be taken into account in this particular process. Phil had wanted to use the new photographs in a poster campaign in the streets of Tripoli and place them in airline magazines, with a caption saying, 'Have you seen this girl?'

These ideas never came to fruition – mainly because Phil was denied access to Libya.]

7 December 2009

The *Inside Out* feature went out this evening in England. It was a great success, apparently, and everyone who saw it thought it went well and could help me find Nadia. Sally Williams sent me a copy and it was really strange, like watching someone else, not me. Mum and Dad did their bit and came across really well. Dad was really emotional in describing his feelings over the last couple of years and said, 'I feel like my heart has been ripped out and Fawzi's trodden all over it.' Phil Owen, now a detective superintendent, was shown in front of the computerised image, which was published for the first time today, exhibiting all his calmness and professionalism on which I had come to rely. Andy Burnham reiterated the diplomatic negotiations and said that he was pleased that I hadn't taken matters into my own hands because it might have changed how the Libyans viewed me. I was really touched when he added, 'I have nothing but respect and admiration for her.' I'm so grateful to everyone involved in this. Phil watched the show with Mum and Dad at their house and apparently they were all in tears, watching me pour my heart out. Although an image of me was in their sitting room, I was all those miles away, with no idea when I'd be back.

Mum and Dad were also interviewed on the BBC *Breakfast* programme, too.

15 December 2009
Andy Burnham rang to say that he had called Tony Blair, who is now special envoy to the Middle East, to raise the issue again. Andy's brilliant at keeping the pressure up.

18 December 2009
There have been more meetings between British Embassy staff and al-Obeidi, who, although sympathetic, has told Vincent that they are treading carefully as Fawzi is unpredictable and they are still concerned for Nadia's safety. She hasn't been seen for so long. Maybe I've been fooling myself, and I will never see her again.

CHAPTER 9

Can We Throw Snowballs at Grandad?

On the evening of 20 December 2009, I received a phone call from Vincent Fean, asking me to be at the British Embassy the following morning at 10am. Together, we would go to meet Mr al-Obeidi, who wanted to see us urgently. This sounded important. Did he have news for me and was it positive, or yet more heartbreak? I didn't sleep very well that night, wondering what it was all about.

I've always been punctual when meeting people and, in Libya, I made sure that I was early for every meeting or court hearing. I only ever missed that one time, which wasn't my fault, and I was usually twenty minutes early. Vincent, Yousef, the interpreter, and I went to al-Obeidi's office, which was just around the corner from the Embassy. As we walked into the office, all the staff smiled at me and acknowledged my presence. They seemed to know me by now – of course, they were all men, just as in the courts. This didn't faze me any more. We waited around for a while and then Ajah arrived with a colleague. Through Yousef, they advised us that they had footage of a girl who they thought was Nadia and wanted me to view the film to confirm it was her.

On a desk in front of me was a laptop and one of the men started to download a file. It seemed like we were waiting forever for the images to take shape on the screen, but at last a figure formed and there was a little girl in a hijab. She was coming out of school with Fawzi's sister Mufeda; she was laughing and seemed happy. I swear my heart stopped beating for a moment. It was her! It was definitely my darling Nadia, who I hadn't seen for over two years. She looked just the same, although obviously older. I started to cry and everyone around me smiled because they knew from my reaction that it was her. I think they were all just as happy as I was.

Although thrilled, I felt a million miles away from Nadia and was inevitably concerned that things could still go wrong. After calming myself down, I asked the interpreter to tell the security men that they must act quickly because I knew Fawzi's brother had a friend who worked for the police and it was he who had been warning Fawzi of their proposed actions. If Fawzi was to get another tip-off, Nadia would once more be moved and I might never see her again.

I was informed that the authorities were fully aware

that they had to move swiftly and reassured that I would very soon have my daughter back. I'd heard all this before, so I wasn't convinced. I informed Yousef of my concerns in no uncertain terms! Yousef told Ajah that Fawzi was a slippery customer and confirmed that he definitely had an informant in the police department. Twice before, we had had sightings of Nadia but, as soon as he had realised that the ESO were onto him, Fawzi had moved Nadia, or changed the route to and from school.

Vincent asked when it would be likely that I would have Nadia back and was told, 'In the next twenty-four hours.' *Twenty-four hours is far too long, especially if Fawzi really does have people in the police tipping him off*, I thought. Vincent stated that we wanted Nadia back that day.

Ajah stated that, now I had confirmed it was Nadia, they would have to get permission from their superior and, once they received the necessary approval, they could move fast. In the next few minutes, Ajah made a few phone calls but nothing more was said to me about what was going on. Vincent reassured me that he felt things were different and he was sure the Libyan police wouldn't slip up again. He told me to go home and pack a few things together; once I got Nadia back, we were to be placed in a secure house for a while until further plans could be laid. Vincent promised that he would call as soon as there was any news.

I wanted to stay and await developments, but I realised Vincent was being sensible; I needed to get ready to meet

Nadia. I was dropped off at my flat, and I ran up the stairs. My heart was pounding heavily as I packed my stuff and most of Nadia's presents and clothes. It was a very strange time and I looked at the flat in a completely different light – it was how people describe an out-of-body experience and I felt like I was looking from above down at my living accommodation and my few meagre possessions.

Nadia started school every day at 1pm and I worked out that if the ESO acted immediately, as they promised, I should be getting a phone call very soon. But then again, if no one contacted me by 2pm yet another opportunity would have been lost. I might be running out of chances to get Nadia back.

At 1.30pm, the telephone rang and I nearly jumped out of my skin! It was Vincent. He told me that a driver from the Embassy would be coming to collect me. I could barely bring myself to find the words for the question that I'd been asking for the last two years, but somehow I managed to gasp, 'Have they found Nadia?'

'Yes, not only have they found her but she's at the police station waiting for you!' was Vincent's calm reply.

I screamed with excitement – I couldn't believe that I would see her soon! For four years, this was the day I'd been longing for. Then my other thoughts turned to my ex-husband: I knew Fawzi would be furious.

I had a little panic when I suddenly thought that I had been mistaken – maybe it wasn't Nadia after all. Perhaps it was some other little girl. No, I was sure it was my girl. Would she remember me? What if she didn't? What would happen? How would I feel? How would *she* feel? I didn't want her to be upset – this experience must be so traumatic for her. All these questions and thoughts were going round in my head and I couldn't think straight. Then I had a brainwave: I remembered the clothes I was wearing the day Nadia was taken and I put them on – specifically to remind her of 'Mummy'. I thought I had better apologise to Vincent for my peculiar attire – not at all respectable – a red hoodie and old black jogging pants tucked into some UGG boots. Normally, I liked to look smart when I visited important people, but this time I didn't care: this time they were getting Nadia's mummy.

The car arrived and took me to the Embassy to pick up Vincent. As I explained earlier, I was convinced that the greengrocer underneath where I lived was a confederate of Fawzi's and was watching my every move. I didn't want to be seen leaving my home with luggage, which might give the game away, so I hid on the floor in front of the back seat, where I couldn't be seen.

This wasn't very dignified but my worries were confirmed when, on the way to the police station, the driver received a phone call from the police, asking if we were in a secure vehicle as they had received information that Fawzi and his brother were driving around the area. The driver told them we weren't in an armed vehicle, to which he was advised to be very careful. I was sitting in the back of the car with Vincent and at one stage had my head in my hands and must have looked worried. Vincent noticed and gave me a hug, and said, 'Well done, you've done it!' *Not yet*, I thought. *Not yet*.

As we drove into the police station car park, the imposing steel security gates closed quickly behind us; that felt safer. We were ushered into an office I had been in before, only this time there were about thirty police officers waiting for me! It made me feel very important, but I had barely entered the room when I asked where Nadia was. One of the officers told me to be patient. *Unbelievable! What a joke – I'd been patient for years!* I asked Vincent to check if Nadia had been informed of what was happening and whether she knew she would be seeing me again. Vincent asked Yousef to see Nadia and make sure she was okay. He returned five minutes later and announced that she was fine. I was now getting desperate – I couldn't work out why I wasn't allowed to see her yet.

I was about to raise hell when – and I can obviously remember the exact time – at 2.30pm, on 21 December 2009, almost two years to the day when I had last seen her, Nadia walked into the room, accompanied by a female plain-clothes officer. There she was! No longer a toddler, she had grown up into a little girl but she was still my baby. She was standing right in front of me, but I wasn't sure what to do. I didn't want to overwhelm her and tried to remember what the child psychologist had advised about taking things steadily.

I just wanted to pick Nadia up in my arms and never let go, but instead I knelt down in front of my daughter and told her that I was her mummy. She nodded shyly. I couldn't hold my emotions in check any longer and started sobbing my heart out. We had finally been reunited! Nadia was a little bewildered and kept repeating in Arabic that she needed to go back to school; she had left her bag at school and was concerned she wouldn't get it back. She was upset, saying that, if she didn't go back to school, the teacher would hit her. This made me so angry and I reassured her that everything would be okay, and she would not be punished. (I later discovered that Nadia was regularly beaten by the teacher at school: if she was late, missed classes or did something wrong, she was slapped on the face or smacked on the hand with a length of hosepipe.)

Nadia asked to see Fawzi and all I could say was that 'the big people' (the police) had said it was best for her to stay with me. This was translated to Nadia because the last thing I wanted was for her not to know what was going on. She had obviously not been speaking English for the last few years – something I had prepared myself for and fully expected – and I didn't want her to feel I was keeping anything from her. One of the police officers asked if this was my daughter. *Do they really think I would be in tears and hugging a complete stranger if this wasn't Nadia?* I thought to myself. I confirmed it was Nadia. Then another officer asked Nadia who I was, to which she replied: 'Mama Sarah.' Those were the words I'd been longing to hear for what seemed a lifetime.

Some of the tough Libyan secret police agents were in

tears and started to take photographs of us. I told them to stop. This was an incredibly emotional personal time for us – the last thing I wanted was to have strangers taking snaps. They did as I asked.

I was then asked to sign some papers, the wording of which Yousef translated for me, and I had to place my thumbprint on a document, confirming that Nadia was now in my care and custody. There were no other formalities and it was time for us to return to the British Embassy. There were police officers in attendance: one or two of them were female, but they were mainly male. Some of them looked pretty serious, which made me a little nervous. To make matters worse, I was then made aware that Fawzi and his brothers were in two separate cars, patrolling the neighbourhood. We were told to be careful, although I wasn't sure what we were meant to do. I now felt even more anxious because I knew Fawzi and his family were capable of anything.

Three unmarked cars were provided for us: the first car was occupied by police and security men. I was in the back of the second vehicle with Nadia and the female police officer; the driver had a police officer next to him. The third car, which was behind us, contained Vincent and two more agents. I should have been calmed by all the muscle, but I wasn't.

The steel gates suddenly opened and our little convoy departed the car park. As soon as we left the safety of the police station, I started to look around nervously for Fawzi, or any cars that might be trailing us. All seemed okay as we sped on our way, and I began to relax slightly – my mistake.

We were about five minutes away from the Embassy when there was a screeching of tyres and a car came hurtling out from a side street. Our driver swerved as the car tried to ram us; I screamed. Luckily, the driver in the car behind had seen what was happening and reacted swiftly by pulling right in front of us to block off the attackers. But that didn't stop them: I could see Fward was in the driving seat and, as the car came to a halt, Fawzi's younger brother got out, brandishing a four-foot iron bar. He rushed up to our car and then launched the weapon at our windscreen. I pushed Nadia to the floor and we all ducked instinctively.

Fortunately, the glass didn't break, but Fawzi's brother then attempted to open the back doors; he was trying to get at Nadia. Our driver suddenly came to his senses, used a central-locking device to secure all the doors and then put the car in reverse, did a U-turn and we were off at high speed. Fawzi's brothers jumped back into their car and drove off quickly before any of our minders could do anything. I gave our driver directions to the Embassy because he didn't seem to know where he was going, and then I noticed that we were being followed by another car – not one of ours. I shouted to our driver to go faster. Nadia was crying, but obviously didn't really know how much danger we were in.

It was like being in the middle of an action movie as we raced along the back streets of Tripoli, in what had now become a car chase. I don't know what had happened to other cars in our convoy – we seemed to be on our own now. Our car really opened up, and the two officers switched on the sirens and flashing lights. We belted through several red lights and stop signs without any concern for pedestrians or other traffic. For once, I approved. Luckily, we were not far from the Embassy and the man riding shotgun – I'm sure he must have been armed – rang ahead so that the gates of the British compound were already opening in readiness for our arrival. Fawzi's brothers gave up at this point and drove away. Soon afterwards, Vincent's car came hurtling through the gates, which then closed swiftly: we were safe!

We got out of the cars and made sure everyone was okay. Nadia was upset, but okay, and we went inside to recover from the ordeal. Anne Otman and Joyce came over to help Nadia and I communicate. Nadia seemed to be more upset at missing school than all the drama of the car chase. She did say that she wanted to see 'Baba', her daddy. Anne explained to her that the police and people in charge thought it best for her to live with Mummy for the time being. She told Nadia that her mummy loved her very much and had been in Libya for over two years, looking for her; she needed to understand that I wasn't taking her away from her daddy forever and she would see him soon. It was also explained to Nadia that she didn't need to worry about returning to school because there were school holidays the following week. Nadia smiled and started to relax, then we played chase and hide and seek around the

Ambassador's swimming pool. Now Nadia was laughing – it was such a relief to see her so happy.

Nadia couldn't believe all the space she had to run around in, and, when I suggested going inside, she refused, wanting to stay outside! She also asked Joyce who she would be sleeping beside that first night. Joyce explained that Nadia would be right next to me and Nadia replied, 'Good!' I was thrilled – we had only been reunited a few hours and she already wanted to be with me. We were bonding quickly – it was a great feeling.

I couldn't wait to call home and managed to get through to my mum. 'Mum,' I announced proudly, 'I have your granddaughter here!' Mum couldn't believe it and then promptly burst into tears. I told her that we were at the Embassy, for now, but would be moved to a safe house soon.

It was then that Vincent informed me that Fawzi and a crowd had started gathering outside the Embassy compound about half an hour after we had arrived. There were now about forty members of his family and friends, all yelling and banging on the gates, demanding entry. I could hear them screaming Nadia's name and it was becoming quite frightening. Vincent thought it was best if we stayed inside. He assured me that we were safe – there were security men all around the grounds of the residence and no one would be able to get at us. I was even more reassured when he told me security outnumbered the mob by more than two to one.

Kalifa, head of the security guards, went out to face the

crowd with some of his men. Fawzi squared up to him, but Kalifa kept incredibly calm and told him to disperse the crowd. Fawzi told Kalifa that as a Libyan he should be on his side, not sticking up for the British. The women were all shouting at Kalifa and shouting about me and Nadia. Kalifa later told me that some of the language the women were using was horrible, and he added, 'No women should say these words about another woman.' He never said exactly what 'these words' were, but it was probably nothing that I hadn't already heard from some of the Libyan men and women when they see a Western woman walking down the street.

Fawzi and his supporters remained outside the residence for about five hours, until he and his brother were taken away. The rest of the crowd were told that they would also be arrested if they didn't go home immediately. Within ten minutes, they had disappeared.

Vincent and the diplomatic staff realised that we were now very much at risk and, to provide us with added protection, we were moved from our intended accommodation in the compound to the Ambassador's residence, Vincent's house, in the main Embassy building.

Nadia was a little upset and, before going to bed, had asked in Arabic to see her daddy. She couldn't understand my English, although I tried to explain why that was impossible. I did my best to tell her that we would see her daddy soon – I wasn't sure if she understood me but she did, at least, stop crying. I ran Nadia a bath and I so enjoyed being with her, doing normal mother-and-daughter stuff. Nadia liked being in the bath. She was becoming more talkative and I could guess the gist of what she was talking about, but it must have been frustrating for her because I couldn't respond in Arabic. However, when I gave her instructions she seemed to know what I was saying and did as I asked. She was amazing! It's almost as if she had stored all her English words in a box at the back of her head and was now bringing them out again.

I woke the next morning with Nadia beside me. *Bliss, just bliss!*

Nadia slept soundly, but despite my happiness I was feeling very unsettled after the demonstration. I was sure we would be at risk – even in the safe house where we were meant to be moving to next. I wouldn't be able to work, and Nadia certainly couldn't go to school; we just wouldn't be able to live a normal life. Still, I had to take one day at a time, and that particular day was lovely: Nadia was pretty content and seemed remarkably settled. She was able to explore the garden, which made her feel more liberated. Via Anne, she told me that she liked being with me because I let her play outside. I rang home again and this time Nadia spoke to Mum and Dad on the phone. They were trying to get a flight to see us both, but it wasn't definite as money was tight and flights were more expensive at Christmas.

There was another telephone call that I also wanted to make that particular day. It was my brother Andy's birthday, and I really wanted Nadia to speak to him. It was difficult for them to understand each other, but it didn't matter. Andy hadn't communicated with Nadia for over two years and he became very emotional. When I spoke to Andy, he told me the family were still coming to terms with what had happened, but they were all celebrating like mad – 'We still can't believe it. History has been rewritten!'

Andy later told me that, as he drove along the M55 motorway in Lancashire, he was in floods of tears, but knew this would always be his best birthday ever.

I wanted Nadia to be able to talk to me about anything, as I had the impression she wasn't allowed to even mention my name when living with Fawzi and his family. In time, Nadia explained that she had asked Fawzi, his mum and his sister where I was and was told that her mummy was in England. They clearly didn't want her to know I was close at hand and were hoping that, in time, Nadia would forget all about me.

A couple of days after I'd been reunited with Nadia, I was able to express my gratitude to all those who had helped me; a report appeared in the *Guardian*. I described Andy Burnham as a 'tower of strength' and I thanked 'the Prime Minister, David Miliband and his team at the Foreign & Commonwealth Office, and the British Embassy in Tripoli, led by Vincent Fean and Arvinder Vohra, for all they have done and are doing to help Nadia and me'.

Andy Burnham was quoted as saying, 'We have waited a long time for this moment, and it has been a very hard road for Sarah. She has shown extraordinary courage, dignity and patience and has lived through any parent's worst nightmare. It has finally come to an end, and I have nothing but admiration for the way she has fought her case in the most trying of circumstances imaginable.' He added, 'Many people have helped to bring this result about, and I would like to thank all of those who have been working tirelessly behind the scenes to make it possible, particularly the British Ambassador and his team. I hope people will now give Sarah and Nadia the time and space to get to know each other again after such a long time apart.'

Phil Owen stated that it had been a 'tortuous' two years and brought to an end two years of worry, heartbreak and upheaval for me and my family: 'They can now concentrate on becoming a complete family again.'

The next couple of days were spent mainly sorting out Christmas and, to add to our excitement, I found out that Andy Burnham had also been helping Mum and Dad again in sorting out the visas they required to visit Libya. This usually took a bit of time, especially during the holidays, but, thanks to Andy, all the bureaucracy had been sorted out for them and they were due to arrive the next day, Christmas Eve, at 8pm. For the last couple of years I hadn't celebrated Christmas, but, once Nadia was with me, I wanted to pull out all the stops.

There was a huge tree and lots of decorations around the house. Nadia was intrigued by all the festivities and, of course, couldn't remember the first few Christmases spent at home. We also had to explain who Father

Christmas was! That night, I put all Nadia's presents I had saved for her over the last few birthdays and Christmases under the tree – I wasn't sure if she fully understood what was going on, but I just wanted to spoil her. We got on really well for those first few days, and I was trying so hard to be the mummy she knew before she was taken. I felt that some of her memories of our life in Wigan were coming back – we just needed to keep spending time together and continue with the bonding.

There was one thing that was worrying me, however. The potentially violent demonstration by Fawzi and his family made it quite clear to me that Nadia and I would be in danger if we were to stay in Libya. We could no longer remain in this country and would have to leave as soon as possible. However, Nadia was still subject to the Sharia law court ruling and, although I had been given custody and now actually had Nadia with me, she wasn't allowed to leave the country.

I discussed this with Vincent and he agreed with me that our safety could now never be guaranteed, no matter where we were in Libya. Fawzi wasn't going to give up on Nadia, and he wasn't going to be pleased with what I had done. We realised that our next move would be vital: we mustn't alienate the Libyan authorities but, at the same time, we needed to be firm in our requests. If possible, we wanted to request special dispensation from the courts to leave Libya.

Vincent was due to meet with Mr al-Obeidi. He thought that he would 'test the waters' to see what his opinion was about our situation and ask whether he would support a request for Nadia and me to return to the UK. It was now make-or-break time, our future was entirely in the hands of the Libyan authorities. If they refused us leave to exit the country legally, then we would have to do a runner, which could be very dangerous. We would also have to wait a long time for things to die down before anything was attempted.

Again there was an anxious waiting period, but Vincent contacted me as soon as he could after the meeting to say al-Obeidi had agreed that the best option for Nadia and me would be to return to the UK. This was brilliant news and a great step forward but Vincent warned that, although al-Obeidi had influence, he still didn't have the final say. He had asked Vincent to get me to write a letter, stating exactly what my fears were about continuing to live in Libya and my thoughts about Nadia's possible abduction, should we remain in Tripoli. Al-Obeidi had stated that he thought Fawzi was nothing more than a criminal and would add his support to the letter, which would be sent to Colonel Gaddafi. I also told Vincent that Mum and Dad were prepared to go and see the Leader and thank him in person for his support.

Christmas Day 2009 was my favourite ever! I had my daughter beside me and my parents were on their way to Libya – nothing else mattered. I woke Nadia up pretty early and told her that Father Christmas had visited. I'd been trying to explain to her all about Father Christmas and always believed that it was important that she was aware of both Christian and Muslim cultures. Nadia was still a little sleepy but we went downstairs. The house was almost empty because everyone had gone to church. That was one thing I had wanted to do – either attend a service on Christmas Day or Midnight Mass on Christmas Eve, but we weren't allowed to leave the premises. And, in the circumstances, I really didn't want to take any chances: I knew Fawzi was out there and could be watching us. If I'm honest, I felt a little frightened at that time and just hoped that Nadia and I weren't forced to move from the accommodation because I felt safe there.

Nadia opened her presents and looked a little overwhelmed. I don't think she realised that all the presents were for her and she wanted to play with them all at once. The Embassy had its own chef and we were provided with breakfast; we tucked into fresh salmon and strawberries. I even had a glass of champagne! I'd never enjoyed such a delicious and happy breakfast.

Mum and Dad were due to arrive that evening, so we prepared for their arrival. Some months ago, I had bought Nadia a trendy little pink outfit and I dressed her in that. I was pleased that Nadia still liked skirts and dressing up, and she loved her outfit. She wasn't talking much about Fawzi and his family, and I didn't want her to feel she couldn't talk about him, but I didn't mention him and instead tried to take things at Nadia's pace.

There were eleven of us for Christmas dinner, which was a proper traditional meal with all the trimmings. Nadia enjoyed the attention, too. Most of my contacts and friends I had made in Libya were spending the holidays at home, but Anne Otman remained and I was able to spend time with her. She was also very helpful and translated some paperwork for me.

Mum and Dad arrived late that night because the flight was delayed. Good old Vincent collected them from the airport and brought them back to the Embassy. I couldn't wait to see them and wondered whether Nadia would recognise them straight away – it would be lovely if she did. But I needn't have worried: when they got out of the car, we ran over to meet them and, after a moment's uncertainty, her face broke into a huge smile.

I was overwhelmed – it was like the icing on the cake that she had remembered her nana and granddad so fondly. While Nadia was hugging Mum, I was so happy and broke down. I could see the relief on Mum and Dad's faces, too. They spent half an hour with us, took some photographs and then, as it had been agreed that they could stay with Anne for the visit, Hatem (one of the security guards) drove them over to Anne's. I knew that they felt a little at risk and a bit nervous, but no threat of danger was going to prevent them from being reunited with their precious granddaughter.

Mum and Dad came to the Embassy the following morning. Nadia played with them most of the day, and I just breathed it all in: my family was back together again. Nadia was insistent that she wanted to go swimming, but the weather was far too cold for us. Then she asked my dad if he would go with her, and he was like putty in her hands. Inevitably, we all went swimming for the first time (and probably the last!) on Boxing Day.

For the next couple of weeks, Mum and Dad came over every day. We couldn't do very much because we had to stay within the compound grounds, but it didn't matter because we were with each other. We played board games and Nadia played in the grounds. She just loved the freedom to be able to run around everywhere and had so many people she could talk to – in Arabic and English. She loved the attention and made a number of friends in the house. Hatem was her best friend and she spent a lot of time with him. Nadia soon had everyone wrapped around her little finger and she knew it!

New Year's Eve was the happiest celebration. Vincent was brilliant in trying to make things possible for my parents, so far from home, and asked how they would spend a typical New Year's Eve in Wigan. Dad told him that one member of the family would go out of the back door at midnight and have to come round the front, where the door would be unlocked, and he or she would be welcomed into the house and given a drink to toast the New Year. Vincent insisted this was exactly what we would do and so we replicated the tradition nearly 2,000 miles from home! Mum and Dad were really touched by this gesture.

While my parents were with us, I couldn't help but wonder whether we might all be able to go home together. The day after I got Nadia, I handed in her old passport and within four hours was issued with a new one for her. It was amazing really, and led me to believe that we might all be able to leave Libya soon – I just had to wait and see.

During this period, Vincent contacted me to say that Fawzi had been in touch with Mr al-Obeidi, requesting permission for him, his sister and various family members to see Nadia. Naturally, I felt sick to the stomach at this request and wondered what he was up to, but Arvinder was back from England and we all discussed it together. It was far too dangerous to take Nadia outside the Embassy grounds – she would be at risk again. Vincent and Arvinder advised that I should let Fawzi see his daughter because it would look good on my part and show that I wasn't keeping Nadia away from him. And, despite all that had happened, I didn't think it would be fair to deprive Nadia of seeing her dad. Any agreement for access would be done in her best interests – I wasn't doing this for Fawzi. So, I reluctantly agreed and the meeting was arranged at the Embassy on 6 January 2010. I insisted the visit would be on my terms and made certain requirements, which were not to be negotiated. Now Fawzi had to abide by my rules. I said that I wanted lots of security around, there were to be no phone calls made and I stipulated that I wanted an interpreter present, who could translate everything that Fawzi was saying to Nadia. If he were to badmouth me, then the visit would be terminated. All this was to be written down in Arabic and given to Fawzi for him to sign in agreement. If he signed, then he would be allowed to see

Nadia and, if not, he wouldn't be allowed anywhere near her; it was as simple as that.

Fawzi eventually agreed to my terms and the meeting was due to go ahead, as arranged. Mum and Dad were still in Libya on the day of his visit, but were due to return to England the following day. This was a bit of a mixed blessing. Although they had always given me unconditional love and support, I'm sometimes best dealing with these sorts of things by myself. I knew exactly what I needed to do in my head but was feeling pressurised at having to explain myself over and over again. While I fully understood that Mum and Dad only wanted what was best for Nadia and me, their worries were adding to my anxiety. It was therefore agreed that they would stay in a separate room with Arvinder and wait for us there, with Nadia's favourite toy (Josie Jump) and a few games, so when the meeting was over we could distract Nadia with all the things she liked.

I still felt aggrieved that it had taken me nearly three years just to see Nadia, whereas Fawzi was able to request access straight away and we had to respond quickly and positively. Still, I realised that in the long run it was tactically sensible, and I had to think of Nadia. I needed to prove to the Libyans that I was a better person and parent than Fawzi; if I stayed calm and composed, he was more likely to lose his temper. I figured that, with every likely outburst, Fawzi would be damaging his own legal case.

I was assured that all the necessary security measures

had been taken and Fawzi's bag would be checked; he would also be frisked and have to go through a metal detector. There were to be two security guards outside the room and two inside. Joyce would sit with me. Yousef would sit next to Fawzi and Nadia, and listen to what was being said. If there was anything I objected to, the visit would be over.

Before we had even begun, I was told that Fawzi had requested his mother be allowed to talk to Nadia on the phone. Typical – he was already making requests beyond our agreement! If I gave him an inch, he would take a yard and next time he would want all the family there. I told Arvinder that Fawzi was always trying to prove a point; I didn't know how close Nadia might have become to her grandmother but, if it helped her, I wouldn't stand in her way. I settled for a brief phone call. The length of the visit was half an hour and Fawzi had also asked to extend the visit to forty-five minutes. My answer was to see how the meeting went and then decide.

Arvinder waited with Mum and Dad, while Nadia and I went into the large meeting room, where Fawzi and a man from al-Obeidi's office were waiting. Fawzi was very smartly dressed in a sharp suit, with shades resting stylishly on his head. He held a flashy mobile phone – posing as usual. I had told Nadia that she could go and hug her daddy, if she wanted to. This she did and then shed a few tears. Fawzi's eyes also filled up and he seemed genuinely moved. Ridiculously, I began to feel a little guilty; I had done nothing wrong but seeing both of them upset affected me. I tried not to show any emotion.

Fawzi gave Nadia a doll (we later discovered it to be broken) and a few cheap sweets. Joyce told me everything that was being said. Fawzi started making false promises to his daughter; he told Nadia that he would take her to the park the following week and that she would soon return to school. He shouldn't have been saying these things to a six-year-old when he had no idea what was going to happen. Nadia was all excited and I was tempted to intervene, but I kept my mouth shut and thought it was better that everyone there could hear what he was saying.

After fifteen minutes, Fawzi asked if he could telephone his mother. It was explained to him that the call must be brief and that only his mother could talk to Nadia, no one else. Nadia took the phone, but I didn't need an interpreter to realise that she was speaking to several different people and not just Fawzi's mother, as agreed. I wasn't happy – I'd known all along that Fawzi would try to take advantage. I looked at al-Obeidi's man and told him in English to terminate the call because I didn't know what was being said to Nadia. The call was ended and the Minister's representative apologised; he knew exactly why I was so angry.

When the visit was over, Fawzi was led out. Nadia was a little upset, but seemed okay. Mum and Dad came in with Arvinder and we all played the 'spotty dog' game to distract her. I explained to Arvinder what Fawzi had done to try to ignore my wishes. Arvinder assured me that his behaviour and attempts to bend the rules had been noted; he was sure this would work in my favour. I wasn't convinced.

Immediately after the meeting, I felt a little down. I felt guilty for what I was doing to Nadia; I didn't want to prevent her from having contact with her father, but he was not to be trusted. I wanted to hate him, but I didn't. More than anything, I pitied him; he still had this hold over me, and this is what I hated. I wanted this feeling to disappear, and I would have loved him to disappear with it! Mum and Dad were going home on an early flight the next day and I didn't want to say goodbye. I never say goodbye – it's like saying, 'I'll never see you again.' I've never liked saying goodbye and, to this day, I won't say it!

We spent the rest of the day playing outside, distracting Nadia and enjoying the rest of our time together. The outside chance of us all going home together looked as if it was over. That night I reassured Mum and Dad they would see us soon. One way or another, I would get us both back, I promised. Dad became a little upset when they left for Anne's house. As we watched them go, I shed a few tears. We went back into the house and Nadia and I performed our nightly ritual of closing the blinds in all the rooms before going to bed.

The following day, my parents rang from Manchester Airport to say that they had arrived safely. I had hardly put the phone down to them when Vincent told me that Colonel Gaddafi had agreed to see Mum and Dad.

Terrible timing! I was gutted, and, when I rang my parents, they were equally disappointed. I was worried that such an opportunity had been lost but then thought that the Leader already knew exactly what we wanted and hadn't achieved anything on our behalf.

During the next fortnight, Vincent, Arvinder and other diplomatic staff continued to work hard on getting us home, but without anything concrete happening. Despite the fact that Nadia and I were safe, Fawzi continued to fight his corner through the courts. There had been several hearings and, although I continued to have custody of Nadia, he was given automatic access. To my shock, he had applied to have overnight access and all day every Friday. My solicitor, Hanan, managed to adjourn the case because we had to make sure Fawzi would only be allowed supervised access. Although it was unsettling and upsetting to have contact with Fawzi during this period, I wanted Nadia to see her father. I was just terrified that, if he was allowed to see Nadia without some official supervision, he would take her and I would never see her again.

When we did return to court, I was accompanied by Arvinder (Hanan had told me that Fawzi would have an interpreter with him and that the judge would be asking me questions direct). Not for the first time, Arvinder was brilliant, calming me down and helping with the procedures. The judge asked me, via the interpreter, whether it was possible I could reconcile with Fawzi and give our marriage another go. I explained that there was no way because I no longer trusted Fawzi: he had hurt me and his daughter so there was no way I would ever get back with him. I also informed the judge that he had since formed another relationship and was now with someone else – I deliberately mentioned this to show Fawzi and his lawyers that I too had my contacts and knew all about his new love. The judge responded by stating that he had been advised that Fawzi and the woman had now split up. I told him that I knew they hadn't, and reiterated there was no chance of reconciliation. (In Tripoli, I discovered that everybody seemed to know each other's business, there was so much gossip – I had found out all this information from a friend of Sally's.)

The judge then asked me to sign a document to witness what I'd said was true. He then informed the court that he would give us his decision at the end of the day. We returned to the house to await news. Arvinder stuck around for a while, which was great because Nadia liked him being there – he was great company and had fun teasing her affectionately. On the odd occasion, Arvinder also took us out – it was lovely to have a change of scenery, even if it was just a trip to the nearby staff house, where there was a small playground and a swimming pool. It felt safe there because there were bodyguards and plenty of security.

At approximately 1pm, Hanan called me and told me that the judge had made his decision: he had awarded Fawzi access on Fridays from 10am. Nadia was to be picked up from the police station and returned there by

5pm. If he was late in returning her, he would lose all his rights to access. This was to start with immediate effect, although we were given the right to appeal, which would buy us a little more time.

I was distraught: if Fawzi had a whole day with Nadia, he would surely kidnap her once more and make sure I never saw her again. After all this, I couldn't believe what was going to happen; we had to get out of the country – and fast! I wasn't going to let Nadia out of my sight; they would have to throw me in prison.

The next few days were hellish due to the uncertainty of it all, but in the end I didn't have to risk jail. Farouk telephoned me and told me to expect a call from al-Obeidi. I then received a text that said: 'Mrs Sarah, please answer urgent'. I called the number back and was put through to al-Obeidi. He asked me how I was and then said he wanted to have copies of our passports, as they were planning to book two flights. I couldn't believe what I was hearing.

'I beg your pardon,' I said. 'Did you say *flights*? For both of us – Nadia *too*? Flights *home*?'

Al-Obeidi laughed and replied, 'Yes, for both of you! I need the passports urgently.'

I told him that I would get the passports to him as soon as I could, and remembered to ask him when we would be flying. 'In a couple of days,' he told me and, with that, he hung up.

Had I heard correctly? Was this really happening? After all we had been through, the news I'd been longing for came true: Nadia and I were finally going home!

I called Vincent straight away and told him the news. He immediately suggested I didn't tell anyone else apart from those already in the know. When Arvinder came to the house, I gave him a great big hug for all his hard work. He had the passports and gave them to Farouk to take to al-Obeidi's office. Vincent finally arrived, having been out all day, and I greeted him like a long-lost hero. He was with someone who looked rather surprised at my reaction. It turned out to be Vincent's boss!

Arvinder and I had a drink, while Vincent's wife, Anne, was teaching Nadia (she had been having regular English lessons from Anne and was coming along really well). We reminisced over everything that had happened and even managed to laugh about some of the funny things, even some of the setbacks. I couldn't believe it was nearly over. Already I was beginning to look at Libya in a different light – it felt like it was no longer my home.

As we didn't know when we would be leaving, I decided not to tell Nadia straight away. I still had to keep things quiet because Fawzi was unaware that we were leaving and we didn't dare put him on alert. Whatever happened, I didn't want to cut him out of Nadia's life completely, though. I told Vincent that I would agree for Nadia to see Fawzi, if ever he was allowed back in England and that, until she decided for herself which religion to follow, I would tell Nadia as much as I could about Islam. If possible, I would also take Nadia back to Libya once a year.

Fawzi had requested to see Nadia again and I agreed,

but this time I insisted there would be no phone calls during the visit. There was to be the same procedure as before, including the security arrangements. This time, Fawzi was granted an hour and, unbelievably, I felt a little guilty because I knew this would be his last visit with Nadia for a while.

Once again, al-Obeidi's security man accompanied Fawzi and he was just as friendly; he smiled, shook my hand and asked how I was. Fawzi had never liked Arvinder and gave him a frosty glare. A cheerful Nadia walked over to Fawzi and said, 'Hello, Daddy!' Joyce was there to interpret and she laughed at the fact that Nadia was talking in English to Fawzi – I was really chuffed too!

Half an hour into the visit, Fawzi's mobile rang. The security man shook his head, clearly not believing that Fawzi was pushing his luck. But Fawzi answered: it was his mum, wanting to speak to Nadia. Fawzi asked the security man if Nadia could talk to her. Al-Obeidi's man shrugged his shoulders and pointed to Arvinder, who then looked in my direction. I nodded, but said: 'Make it quick!' Nadia was actually on the phone for a while and Arvinder could tell I wasn't happy. The security guy could see that Fawzi had overstepped the mark and instructed him to end the call, which he reluctantly did. Just before the hour was up, Vincent came into the room and called an end to the meeting. Fawzi said his goodbyes to Nadia. There were no tears this time, and Nadia took it all well.

Outside, Vincent showed Fawzi an agreement that had been drawn up, which requested his signature giving permission for Nadia to leave the country in my custody. Fawzi scanned the first line of the document and then simply refused to read any further – never mind give his agreement. He left angrily.

The following day, 11 February, I asked Arvinder if he would take me out to buy Nadia a 'going home' outfit. She was to stay at the Embassy with Joyce. He agreed to take me to various shops, including British Home Stores, Marks & Spencer and Next – all of which had branches in Tripoli. Before we hit the stores, however, Arvinder insisted on taking me for a drink in the Radisson Hotel because he said he needed to update me on what was going on. I started to worry and wondered if there had been a change of plan; perhaps the Embassy staff were too frightened to tell me? Why hadn't he said something before? My uneasiness was further heightened by Arvinder's quiet mood – he said very little in the car on the journey, but advised that he would explain more when we reached the hotel.

We sat down in the Radisson's lounge and Arvinder asked about my plans for when I got home and if I would want much publicity. I hadn't really thought about it and wondered why he was asking me. He was reading an email, and then I noticed that he was holding what looked like tickets in his hand.

'What are those – tickets?' I asked.

'I'm going to Tunis at the weekend.'

'You told me that you were going to Tunis, but I thought you were going by car.'

Arvinder handed me the tickets and said, 'Take a look if you like.'

I opened the envelope and took out the ticket. On it was printed his name but the destination wasn't Tunis: the airline ticket was from Tripoli to London, and then London to Manchester. My heart leapt. Arvinder was coming home with us; he was escorting us home! It was just what I wanted. Arvinder asked if I wanted to see the date, but I didn't care – I just jumped up and hugged him. Our flights were booked! I knew we were going home.

Arvinder explained that we were travelling in two days' time – on Saturday, 13 February. He didn't have the tickets yet – Saif al-Islam, one of Colonel Gaddafi's sons, was sorting them out. Al-Obeidi and Vincent had brought our situation to his attention and he had agreed to try to resolve the matter quickly.

I was buzzing. We went shopping, and I must have been impossible to be with because I was so excited – I'm sure Arvinder was glad to get rid of me at the end of the day! Anyway, I got Nadia a few things and Arvinder bought her a 'Cheeky Monkey' top because that was his nickname for her.

As soon as I got home, I called Mum and Dad to tell them the news. They were over the moon, but I had to tell them not to say a word to anyone apart from Steph and Andy. It was agreed that I would tell Nadia that we were going home the following day, and I wanted Arvinder, Vincent, Anne and Hatem to be present when I told her. I needed Nadia to feel happy about going to England and

I believed that having people around her, who would encourage her and who she knew and liked, would make her feel secure.

The following evening, 12 February to be exact, was when I decided to give Nadia the news. All the people I wanted were there. I had told our security guard, Hatem, earlier in the day. Over the weeks, he had become very close to Nadia, so I felt that I should do the decent thing and tell him we were leaving. He was shocked and even shed a tear. Of course he was pleased for us but obviously sad that we were going. I'd asked him not to say anything to Nadia and he kept our secret.

I sat Nadia down and said that I had something very important to tell her, and she needed to listen to me carefully.

'Okay, Mummy,' she said.

I told her we would be going to England and Daddy wasn't coming, but he could come and see us when we were settled. Nadia nodded and repeated, 'Okay, Mummy,' and then added, 'Can we throw snowballs at Granddad?'

I couldn't believe that Nadia was being so mature about it all – it couldn't have gone better. Throughout the evening, she was talking about England and the snow. I had told her that Arvinder would be accompanying us, and she asked if Vincent, or Anne and Hatem were coming too – she seemed more concerned about leaving them behind than her father! Then I walked Hatem to the door and gave him one last hug. We both burst into tears and he told me to look after Nadia; he would try to visit us in England soon.

Arvinder stayed for dinner and I raised my glass to him and all those who had helped us. After he left, we closed all the blinds as usual. Nadia had a bath and I asked her if she had any questions before we went to sleep. 'No, Mummy,' she replied. 'None.'

The flight home was due to leave at 1pm, but we woke up early in the morning, very excited. I had to go to court first thing in the morning for some kind of formality – signing some document – although I wasn't sure what it was, but I'd been told I had to do it. As long as we were on the flight that afternoon, I didn't care what I had to sign! Vincent, Farouk and I went to a courthouse I'd never been to before. Farouk went inside to see if the judge was ready to see me. He was gone for about twenty minutes and, when he came back, he announced that the judge wasn't releasing any documentation for signature – the judge apparently required Fawzi's signature to issue an order allowing Nadia out of the country. Farouk had tried to explain that this wasn't necessary due to Saif Gaddafi's involvement, but the judge wasn't interested.

The only person who could instruct the judge and override his decision was another Mohammed, Saif's personal assistant, who had been sorting out the paperwork and the tickets. As luck would have it, Mohammed was mid-air on a flight from London and not due back until after our flight was due to take off! I couldn't believe that here was yet another twist in the saga on the very day we had supposedly been granted our freedom. Despite protests from Vincent and Arvinder, the judge refused to budge and we were unable to board our flight.

Embassy staff contacted Mohammed immediately on his return, and he telephoned the judge to explain the situation: Fawzi's permission was not required. Another flight was booked for the following morning at 10am. Although another 'escape plan' had been arranged within twenty-four hours, I was left wondering whether I would ever get out of Libya with Nadia. Even though Fawzi didn't know about our ruse, would an extra day somehow give him the chance to discover what we were doing and find a way of stopping us? Although beside myself with anxiety, I had to remain calm for Nadia's sake. I told her not to worry about the delay – we would be going home soon.

The next morning, we were up even earlier. Surely this must be it? But the time just dragged and when we were still at the Embassy at 9.30am – just half an hour before the flight was due to leave – I started to panic. Arvinder kept telling me not to worry and said they wanted to keep us safe until the last possible minute. At 9.45am, we were given the go-ahead and went outside to find a fleet of police cars waiting. I hadn't been allowed to tell anyone I was leaving, in case Fawzi found out and made trouble at the airport, but I was able to say a proper goodbye to Anne Otman. It was very emotional and both of us broke down as we hugged each other tightly. I had met some wonderful people in Libya, and I felt Anne's support typified all the care and help I had received.

Vincent and his wife Anne accompanied us to the airport and there were more poignant farewells. They had both been amazing to me, and Vincent had gone well beyond the call of duty in his role as British Ambassador – I will never forget him. Nadia and I were then taken to a secluded runway until we boarded the plane just after its scheduled departure time. I felt embarrassed that the flight had been delayed because of us. I'd always been cross with late boarders who left it to the last minute and kept other travellers waiting – now Nadia and I were those inconsiderate people! I also felt a bit awkward at being taken through the plane into Business Class, which I had never been in before. The other passengers must have been annoyed and I wondered if they were thinking, *Who do these people think they are?*

Even after the flight had taken off, I remained very anxious. For almost three years, I had been living on the edge, not knowing what the next hour would bring so I was still half-expecting something to go wrong. I remember sitting on the plane, just after take-off, and looking down at the terrain and saying, in Arabic, 'Goodbye, Libya. Goodbye!' As I said previously, I never say goodbye to anyone because I believe 'goodbye' means you're never going to see them again. On this occasion, I happily said goodbye to Libya.

CHAPTER 10

Wishing on a Star

'The question isn't who is going to let me; it's who is going to stop me.'

Ayn Rand, writer and philosopher

Although we were on our way home, I still couldn't believe the ordeal was finally over. There had been unexpected hitches, delays and even disasters at every turn and I was convinced that somehow the plane would be turned around in mid-air! Fortunately, my fears were unfounded but it was still very difficult to completely unwind.

Nadia, on the other hand, was in great form on the flight home, very excited and full of questions: 'When will we be there?', 'How long will the plane take?', 'Are we in London yet?', 'Are we in England yet?' Arvinder was brilliant with her and very patient for the duration of the flight. No one on the plane knew our story and so, apart from being in Business Class, we weren't treated any differently.

When we landed at Heathrow on Valentine's Day 2010, I remember Arvinder saying to me, 'Here we are, on British soil!' Despite feeling some relief, I thought to myself that I wouldn't really be home until I had my mum, dad, brother, sister and all the family around me. Nadia couldn't quite understand that, when we landed, we weren't in Manchester and had to get another flight, but she was soon distracted and excited by the sight of snow on the ground.

We made our way to the Business Class lounge, where I helped myself to a glass of wine (or three), which helped steady my nerves! To be honest, I still felt a little anxious, although I was grateful knowing all the relatives were waiting for me. I imagined my dad desperately wanting to be at the airport early. In fact, I'm surprised he didn't camp outside the airport all night! (He had actually been at Manchester Airport several hours before my arrival.)

Arvinder asked if he could take Nadia to the shop to buy her some sweets. I must have looked doubtful because he looked at me in a reassuring way and said, 'Don't worry, I'll look after her – she'll be quite safe with me.' I remember laughing and thinking he was one of the people I trusted the most. Of course Nadia would be safe, so I sat back and enjoyed my white wine.

Arvinder rang Vincent and told him we had arrived

safely in London and we were just waiting for our connecting flight. Later, I was told that, after Arvinder's call to Vincent, Farouk telephoned Fawzi to tell him that Nadia and I were in the UK. Fawzi was naturally furious; he threatened Farouk and told him that he would kill ten Libyans and ten English people who had been involved in our return to Britain. I wasn't surprised by his reaction or his threats; I had always been scared of Fawzi's temper, and I had often thought of what he might be capable of if he really became angry with Nadia or me.

The flight from Heathrow to Manchester was scheduled around 1.30pm, or so I thought. I was just settling down to another glass of wine when Arvinder asked me to check the time on the tickets. I took a look and nearly fainted; we were actually due to fly out at 1pm and it was already 12.45pm! We hadn't changed our watches to local time and had lost all track of time. We virtually ran the full length of the airport to our terminal, where the last passengers had already boarded. Then Nadia decided she needed the toilet. I breathlessly explained to the staff who fortunately were very understanding and waited to close the gate until she had been to the bathroom. Having gone through all this, it would have been ironic if we'd missed the flight due to my 'celebrations'. I imagined the headlines...

Anyway, we soon buckled ourselves in and were taking off again on the last leg of the journey. Nadia was still very excited, constantly checking with me that Nana and Granddad would be waiting for us. She wasn't nervous at all, and I think it made a difference that I'd been open and honest with her from the start, so she was always aware of what was happening and what to expect. Arvinder, 'her partner in crime', kept her occupied and they played the 'spotty dog' game quite a few times. Nadia loved Arvinder's company and it helped so much, having him accompany us. Throughout the whole ordeal in Libya, he had been brilliant. My head was all over the place – not just from the wine – and the closer we got to home, the more excited and distracted I became.

We touched down in Manchester and, when we came to a halt, I saw two police Range Rovers on the runway, waiting for us. As we were travelling Business class, we were first off the plane. Arvinder told us to run ahead and the first people I saw were *my* police officer, Phil Owen, and *my* MP, Andy Burnham – the two men who had been steadfast in their attempts to help and support the Taylors over the last few years. I ran into their arms, and immediately burst into tears. There were two police officers, who directed us all to the waiting cars. Andy told me that all my family were waiting for me at the Radisson Hotel, just two minutes from the runway; he also warned me that there was some press there, too.

Phil Owen later told me that our arrival at Manchester was one of the highlights of his police career. All the hard work and commitment had paid off and, standing alongside Andy Burnham on the tarmac when our plane touched down at Manchester Airport, Phil turned to Andy and simply said, 'We've done it!'

When we pulled up outside the hotel, all I could see was Dad pounding down the stairs with about four TV cameramen behind him. Mum was in the toilet and he couldn't wait any longer for her! He threw Nadia up in the air and asked her if she remembered him and her nana; he told her how much he had missed her and then shouted as loud as he could, 'You've done it, Sarah! You've done it, girl!' He was the proudest dad ever. Dad was quickly followed by my brother, Andy, and his wife, Kirsty; Andy was soon hugging and kissing us for dear life. He hadn't seen Nadia for nearly three years and we met his daughter, Frankie, then 18 months old, for the first time. Mum, Steph and Jay joined us and then we all broke down, sobbing with joy and relief.

We made our way into the hotel's conference room, which Phil Owen had hired. As I marched in, punching the air in triumph, the rest of my family and friends were sitting around a table, festooned with balloons and banners and covered in Nadia's toys; they all cheered loudly. My dad was still carrying Nadia and he brought her into the room, where she was greeted with more yells of delight and applause. This was all filmed by the BBC and when I look back at the scene I realise poor Nadia looks quite shell-shocked and overawed. In retrospect, perhaps we should have made the homecoming a more low-key affair for Nadia's sake, but my friends and family had been so supportive and caring that we wanted to share this momentous occasion with them.

There was then a short press briefing and I did a

number of television interviews, where I thanked everyone for their help. Nadia sat on my lap and smiled happily, trying with some difficulty to wink at the camera! Mum ecstatically told the television crews: 'It's the best feeling! We are so happy now we just want to spend some time together alone as a family.'

Andy Burnham was asked to comment and responded by saying: 'Sarah has been travelling alone on the hardest road imaginable for any mother, but she is home tonight and her nightmare is over. Seeing Sarah and Nadia walk together up the ramp at Manchester Airport was an emotional moment that I'll never forget. It is almost three years since Nadia was taken illegally out of the same airport, but tonight she is back where she belongs, supported by a warm and loving family, and a strong close-knit community.'

Even after it was time to leave the hotel, Dad still wasn't going to let us out of his sight now he'd got us back and, despite Phil and the police officers offering to escort us, he insisted on driving us back home. When we finally did arrive home, I saw that they had decorated the front of the house especially for our homecoming. There was a huge sheet on the front window and on it was written, 'WELCOME HOME SARAH AND NADIA'. Balloons were pinned to the gates, too. It was all so perfect.

Once inside, I was struck by the fact that everything was so small because the houses in Libya had very high ceilings and big rooms. Mum and Dad's house looked tiny, but it was home and it was *our* home, so nothing mattered any more. The first thing Dad pointed out for me to sort out, with a twinkle in his eye, was the amount of boxes of possessions they had removed from my old house – at least thirty of them stacked from floor to ceiling in the back bedroom! I was eager to look through them all, to see my own belongings again.

We just sat down and chatted. A few of my cousins came over to join the rest of the family for some celebratory drinks. I recounted my story – as briefly as I could – just outlining the main events, but we were exhausted and soon went to bed. It was heaven to sink into the new bedding that Mum had bought for us! We talked for a while and I asked Nadia, as I still do now, did she have any concerns or worries; was there anything she wanted to talk about? 'No, Mummy, I'm fine,' she replied, and, with that, she went off to sleep almost immediately. As I snuggled beside my princess, still in a state of disbelief that she was next to me, I just stared at her peaceful face: I was at home with Nadia, in our bed, in England, in Wigan!

Nadia was in great spirits the next morning. I repeated that we would now be living in England with her grandparents – something that I had explained to her several times before we left Libya. She was absolutely fine about it all. I told her that eventually we would invite her dad to see her. We talked, and still do talk about Libya – it was our home for three years, and for the first few days that we were home we reminisced quite a lot about our time there. Nadia delighted in all the attention she was receiving and enjoyed answering questions from the family about her time in Tripoli. She did ask me: 'Is my dad going to come for me again and take me to Libya, then will you have to come and get me again?' I tried to reassure her and told her that wouldn't ever happen again; from now on this was her home.

The following day, I started to receive calls from journalists, TV, radio and magazines and we did quite a lot of interviews – some with Nadia. I have to admit, she liked being in the limelight and enjoyed seeing herself on television. She would often ask me, 'Mummy, are we famous now?' I would reply, 'I guess so, darling!' She would walk around town and announce proudly, 'People keep looking at me – that's because we're famous, Mum.' A few people did stop us when we were out and about in Wigan, and would praise me for what I'd done and wish me all the best. I couldn't, and still can't, see the big deal: I did what I had to do as a mum.

A week after our arrival back in England, Mum and Dad organised a few drinks at the house to celebrate our return. Andy Burnham came with his daughters, Rosie and Annie, and Phil Owen attended with his daughter Ellena. They were all so genuinely pleased for us and it was great to see them again. While I was in Libya, Andy had called to tell me that he had been approached by a television agent who was interested in my story and that I should think about it when I came home; he spoke to the agent again and they were still interested in making a film about my fight to get Nadia back. The sense of achievement was amazing, although I never felt I was particularly brave or courageous: all the time it just felt as if it was something in which I had no choice. I had to do it, but the more people talked about it, the more proud I felt. At times I still think about it all and still appreciate being at home with Nadia.

Soon after our return, Donya Al-Nahi got in touch. She said she was thrilled for me, but, to be honest, I didn't feel particularly pleased to hear from her. After all, she had done very little for me while I was in Libya and, although she said that she would be in touch again soon, I didn't hear from her again. In all, since Nadia was first kidnapped, we had paid her a grand total of £21,000. Among other things, this included payment for acquiring a lawyer and monies to people who were supposed to help me and help us get out of the country. Apart from engaging my first lawyer, Mohammed, none of the other help originally promised had actually happened. And during my stay in Libya, I never had any reassurance from Donya or her contacts that Nadia was safe. Looking back, I believe that Donya, who had professed such expertise and support, took advantage of my situation: I was desperate and vulnerable and she knew that I would do anything and pay anything for Nadia's safe return. I never tried to retrieve any of the money – I suppose I could have done, but I was just so relieved to have Nadia back that she was all that mattered.

I've had such an incredible amount of help, support

and love from so many people in England and Libya – the one person who let me down was Donya.

At the end of March, we celebrated the homecoming properly. Andy Burnham hired a room for us at the Monaco Ballroom in Hindley, where we enjoyed a buffet dinner and disco. We sent invites to all our friends and family at home, as well as all those in Libya who had helped us. Over 200 joined us, including Sally and her husband, Abi. I even extended an invitation to Colonel Gaddafi and, although he didn't come, the Leader sent his apologies. Funny when you think of some of the terrible things he perpetuated in his dictatorship for which he never apologised! It was lovely to see all my friends and family again. My friend Leona made the most amazing cake for Nadia – a huge Disney castle, which contained 6lb of flour, butter and sugar, 50 eggs and over 15kg of icing sugar. It was the biggest cake I'd ever seen! I made an emotional speech, thanking everyone who had supported me, and most people were in tears. It was evident that everyone was so relieved and happy that we were back where we belonged.

Nadia actually settled back at home pretty quickly. I thought it was important to get her into a routine as soon as possible, so I enrolled her into the local primary school. We were shown around the school by the head teacher and, to my amazement, we discovered that Jay, Nadia's best friend from her nursery school, was in the same class and asked to look after Nadia, which was great. I made the head teacher aware of our situation and that Nadia needed to be picked up from class by me, Mum or Dad, and that she must never be left in the care of anyone else after school time. The teachers were very understanding and did just as I asked. If Nadia ever goes to university, I'll probably be driving her there and giving the lecturers similar instructions!

In fact, for the first twelve months after our return, we still felt wary and I was very reluctant to leave Nadia on her own. I found myself looking over my shoulder a lot of the time. For three years, I'd been living off adrenaline when every day was stressful, so it was strange to be in an environment where for most of the time we felt able to relax. It was also true that I did feel much safer now that we were living with Mum and Dad. We were advised by the police to install security alarms on the windows and also told that the community police would call round from time to time to check on us. I did have some concerns that Fawzi's friends in England might try something, but I was also a little reassured that they would know how much trouble Fawzi had got himself into, and that they would probably not want to get involved. I just needed to be alert at all times – I still never let Nadia out of our sight.

Phil Owen has been in touch regularly since our return and my dad wrote a letter to the police chief, praising his work and unfailing commitment. I have also maintained contact with Andy Burnham: I was pleased to support his campaign for the leadership of the Labour Party during 2010, and last year Andy came to open a new building in

Nadia's school. He went into one of the classrooms, where he said, 'I think I know someone here.' Nadia immediately shot her arm up in the air and gave Andy a great big smile!

Andy had some further involvement in November 2010 when he received a letter from the Libyan Ambassador, Omar Jelban, referring to a meeting two years previously between them. Mr Jelban stated that the 'happy ending couldn't be reached without good co-operation and the condition that Sarah Taylor would keep bridges open for the girl to return to Libya at least twice a year to visit her father and relatives'. He went on to write that I was in breach of this agreement in refusing to travel to Tripoli, dismissing the fact that Fawzi had threatened me and reported that 'the Libyan authorities' assurance to provide protection and assistance to Sarah, as well as a safe return, had been ignored'. He was also of the opinion that 'annual visits are beneficial to Nadia's well being, socially and psychologically, to help heal past injuries'.

In the beginning of 2011, Andy replied to Jelban, advising him that I had made a number of offers for Fawzi to visit the UK, none of which had been taken up. Andy quite rightly didn't even address the possibility of Nadia and I returning to Libya. There was no question of that happening, no matter how much the Libyans were committed to our safety. Of course, just a few months later, the situation in Libya changed forever with the revolution to oust Colonel Gaddafi.

In May 2011, Omar Jelban was ordered to leave the UK, following attacks on the British Embassy in Tripoli. This was as a result of NATO air strikes on the capital. I was horrified when I heard that the building had been completely burned down, but fortunately all my friends and contacts had already been withdrawn. Vincent Fean was later posted to Jerusalem as Consul General and Arvinder returned to London.

As regards some of my other contacts in Libya, they were all affected by the revolution: Nuri Al-Mismari sought asylum in France. Abdul Ati al-Obeidi was detained west of Tripoli by rebel forces and is currently in prison. Gaddafi's son Saif al-Islam, who paid for our air tickets out of Libya, attempted to flee the country disguised as a Bedouin tribesman and at the time of writing is being held captive in the mountain town of Zintan and likely to be tried for crimes against humanity. I guess we all know of Colonel Muammar Gaddafi's fate.

My heart runs cold when I think of what might have happened if all the efforts to bring Nadia home had failed in 2010. A year later, the terrible truth is that it would have been highly dangerous for me to remain in Libya during the uprising and the ensuing civil war. To have located Nadia and brought her home without assistance from British and Libyan authorities would, I'm sure, have proved impossible.

Unfortunately, my experience of having a child snatched and taken abroad is not so uncommon as you might think. In 2008 alone (the most current figures available), there were about 500 children abducted. Such incidences usually occur following the breakdown of a marriage when the parent who is not awarded custody kidnaps their child. The government has little power to intervene in around 40 per cent of these cases as they have been taken to countries not signed up to the 1980 Hague Convention, an international treaty obliging nations to return children wrongfully retained in their jurisdiction. Libya is one of those countries that have still not signed up to the Convention. With more and more transcultural marriages taking place, there is also likely to be an increase in child abductions.

I was told, and experts confirm, that it is almost impossible for mothers to get back children taken by their fathers to Islamic countries with Sharia law. In fact, I was the first mother to successfully bring a child back from Libya legally. The sad thing is I'm one of the lucky ones – there are so many parents out there who haven't got their children back. They must never give up hope; it can be done.

The patriarchal culture still prevails; it seems that it is okay for men like Fawzi to enjoy the decadent lifestyle of the West and have sex with European women but then they disapprove of their offspring doing the same and want their own children (especially girls) raised in the Muslim faith. I have no problem with my daughter following a specific faith and have always thought it was important for Nadia to choose her own religion. If she decided to become a Muslim, then I would certainly respect that decision. She has a headscarf, which she can wear when she wants, and we keep a Koran in the house. I would also arrange for her to attend the necessary Islamic classes, should she choose to do so in the future.

I have always tried to be honest with Nadia and to put my own feelings to one side when we have talked about her father. Of course, I would be more than happy never to have to set eyes on Fawzi ever again, but I have to think of Nadia. He is still her father, no matter what he has done and I know I couldn't have lived without my own dad. I'm very open with Nadia, and I think this is important. She is old enough now to understand for herself what has happened. I have asked Fawzi to come and visit Nadia on several occasions and each time he has failed to apply for a visa. Apparently, he demanded bodyguards and a private jet to bring him to the UK and, when this was refused, he blamed me for not making it happen. Up until a few months ago, he had an open offer (without private jet) to come here, but the situation has changed again since then. At the time of writing, Fawzi has started making new death threats to people in Libya and has singled out my lawyer for special attention. Now, I really have to consider what's best for Nadia and I cannot put her in any more danger. Nadia is amazingly mature for her age and seems to understand the situation. Perhaps, in time, when she is an adult, she might wish to visit her Libyan family and I would, of course, support her, although I'm sure I would worry the whole time she was there.

I think it's very important to be honest with your child. Nadia has been through so much that I felt that I had to tell her the truth about everything that has happened. My mum and dad were always open and honest with me when I was sick as a child – I want Nadia to feel like that with me and I don't want her to feel that she can't approach me and speak to me about anything. I'm her mum and I'll do anything to put things right for her.

We do still talk about Fawzi, and she continues to ask me why he did what he did. I can only say that I really don't know. There are some questions she asks me that I truly can't answer; I tell her to write them down and one day she may be able to ask him herself. Occasionally, she does tell me that she misses her dad and we sit down and talk about him. I tell her that her dad still loves her and, as much as I want to, I try not to badmouth him in front of her. We also own a 'worry box' – an old shoebox that we have decorated. If either of us feels worried or upset about anything, we write our concerns on a piece of paper and place it in the box to take out and discuss when we feel we need to. I'm glad to say that it isn't being used as much these days as when we first came home.

Nadia wasn't allowed to talk about me when she was in Tripoli, but her dad and his family couldn't stop her thinking about me. She always remembered the little gesture we did together when we would point to her head and heart and repeat, 'Mummy is always in your heart and in your head,' but there was something else that linked Nadia to us, all those miles away.

Wishing on a Star

While Nadia and I were still separated in Libya, back in Wigan my dad used to go into his garden and scour the night sky despondently. He focused upon the nearest star, and wished and wished for Nadia's safe return. Nearly 2,000 miles away, under African skies, Nadia regularly looked up at the brightest star and repeated to herself: 'Please, star, tell the moon to tell Mummy where my dad's hiding me so she can come and find me.'

And that's exactly what I did.